S0-BRR-940

THE PROBLEM OF HISTORY
IN MARK

STUDIES IN BIBLICAL THEOLOGY

A series of monographs designed to provide clergy and laymen with the best work in biblical scholarship both in this country and abroad

Advisory Editors:

C. F. D. MOULE, *Lady Margaret's Professor of Divinity in the University of Cambridge*

JAMES BARR, *Professor of Semitic Languages and Literatures,
University of Manchester*

PETER ACKROYD, *Samuel Davidson Professor of Old Testament Studies,
University of London*

FLOYD V. FILSON, *Professor of New Testament Literature and History,
McCormick Theological Seminary, Chicago*

G. ERNEST WRIGHT, *Professor of Old Testament History and Theology
at Harvard University*

STUDIES IN BIBLICAL THEOLOGY· 21

THE
PROBLEM OF HISTORY
IN MARK

JAMES M. ROBINSON

Emory University

SCM PRESS LTD
BLOOMSBURY STREET LONDON

THIS STUDY WAS AWARDED A PRIZE IN THE
1954-5 COMPETITION SPONSORED BY THE
CHRISTIAN RESEARCH FOUNDATION

SBN 334 01309 7

FIRST PUBLISHED 1957
SECOND IMPRESSION 1962
THIRD IMPRESSION 1968

PRINTED IN GREAT BRITAIN
BY PHOTOLITHOGRAPHY
UNWIN BROTHERS LIMITED, WOKING AND LONDON

226.3
R66p
c. 2

CONTENTS

LIST OF ABBREVIATIONS

BJRL	*Bulletin of the John Rylands Library*
ET	*Expository Times*
HNT	*Handbuch zum Neuen Testament*
JBL	*Journal of Biblical Literature*
JBR	*Journal of Bible and Religion*
JTS, n.s.	*Journal of Theological Studies*, new series
MEYER	*Kritisch-Exegetischer Kommentar über das Neue Testament*, begründet von H. A. W. Meyer
NTD	*Neues Testament Deutsch*
SJT	*Scottish Journal of Theology*
Str-B	Strack-Billerbeck, *Kommentar zum Neuen Testament aus Talmud und Midrasch*
TB	*Theologische Blätter*
TLZ	*Theologische Literaturzeitung*
TR, n.F.	*Theologische Rundschau*, neue Folge
TSK	*Theologische Studien und Kritiken*
TWNT	*Theologisches Wörterbuch zum Neuen Testament* ed. by G. Kittel and G. Friedrich
ZNW	*Zeitschrift für neutestamentliche Wissenschaft*
ZST	*Zeitschrift für systematische Theologie*
ZTK	*Zeitschrift für Theologie und Kirche*

I

THE PROBLEM OF HISTORY IN THE INTERPRETATION OF MARK

A. THE NINETEENTH CENTURY: MARK AS IMMANENT, OBJECTIVE HISTORY

The traditional view of Mark as an abridgement of Matthew is responsible for the general neglect of Mark throughout the ages. But once the priority of Mark had become apparent,[1] interest in the historical Jesus rapidly directed attention to Mark. Since the earliest record is nearest the events themselves, it is most likely to have access to reliable sources (Papias pointed to Peter), and to be free from subsequent interpretation, legend-building and allegorizing (contrast John). Furthermore one proof of Marcan priority consisted in evidence that Matthew and Luke reworded Marcan stories, so that the literary personalities and theological biases of Matthew and Luke became apparent. Since there was no earlier source with which Mark could be compared, the illusion of a Marcan simplicity, neutrality, and objective historicity arose. Thus literary criticism pointed the way for the first period in Marcan interpretation.

The literary question of the interrelations among the synoptic Gospels was overshadowed by the historical issue posed by David Friedrich Strauss' *Leben Jesu* in 1835. It became necessary to prove the historicity of Jesus. The various implications of the Marcan priority for its objective historicity now came into conscious consideration, and the 'Marcan hypothesis' entered into general acceptance as a combination

---

[1]The first evidence that Matthew uses Mark was supplied by Christian Gottlieb Wilke in 1826 in an article 'Über die Parabel von den Arbeitern im Weinberge Matth. 20.1–16', in Winer's *Zeitschrift für wissenschaftliche Theologie*, I, 73–88. The basic argument from order, to the effect that Matthew and Luke follow the same order only when parallel to Mark, was provided by Carl Lachmann, 'De ordine narrationum in evangeliis synopticis', *TSK*, VIII (1835), 570–90. Further proof from a detailed analysis of form was provided by Wilke in *Der Urevangelist*, 1838.

of two motifs: Marcan priority and Marcan objective historicity.[1] The desired reconstruction of the historical Jesus in terms of character development, psychological comprehensibility, and 'historical probability' found in Mark its documentary proof; and Mark found, through identification with this reconstruction, the proof of its objective historical character.[2]

The general assumption at the end of the nineteenth century as to Mark's understanding of history was to the effect that Mark regarded history as a series of objective events in an empirical relationship of cause and effect. The various aspects of the Marcan narrative which do not fit such a pattern can be disregarded as due to the fact that Mark was not yet a thoroughly enlightened man. The few theological (Pauline) influences can be easily identified and discounted. Such non-historical vestiges do not point toward a completely different understanding of history; they are not the points which provide the key to the whole. Rather the Marcan history is immanent and understandable in its presuppositions and intentions. Therefore a critical sifting and purification of the record does not eliminate any of the truth of history, but rather rescues what truth is present in Mark's history.

Upon this secular definition of the truth of history there was superimposed a religious, Ritschlian definition: the truth of history consists in the moral truths revealed through the teachings and examples of great men. Thus Jesus' teachings are of higher value than his action. His action is to be correlated with truth by finding in it motives or intentions which can be translated into moral principles or objectives. History has meaning as the laboratory in which truth is discovered; once the truth has been grasped and communicated to posterity, the history itself ceases to be of decisive importance. Mark tells Jesus' story to propagate the truths he learned from Jesus.

---

[1]This pattern was initiated by Christian Hermann Weisse, *Die Evangelische Geschichte kritisch und philosophisch bearbeitet*, 1838, and dominated the interpretation of Mark down to Heinrich Julius Holtzmann. Holtzmann provided in *Die synoptischen Evangelien*, 1863, both the most masterly proof of the priority of Mark and the most successful presentation of the historical Jesus, thus apparently proving the case for the objective historical accuracy of Mark.

[2]For the many Ritschlian lives of Jesus which are but variants of Holtzmann's synthesis, cf. Schweitzer, *The Quest of the Historical Jesus*, 193 ff. For the persistence of this approach into the following period cf. Ebeling, *Das Messiasgeheimnis und die Botschaft des Marcus-Evangelisten*, 19 ff.

B. THE TURN OF THE CENTURY: MARK AS NON-HISTORICAL THEOLOGY

A new tack in the interpretation of Mark was inaugurated[1] by the appearance in 1901 of Wrede's *Das Messiasgeheimnis in den Evangelien*. The basic insight of Wrede is that Mark is not a transparent medium through which the historical Jesus can be easily seen. Rather Mark is a prism which must be analysed in and of itself, before conclusions can be drawn as to the historicity of what is recounted. Only by discounting the point of view and prejudice of the author can the objective historian hope to establish the real facts of Jesus' life lying behind the Marcan narrative. Wrede observed that the historical and psychological reasoning which was generally assumed to characterize Mark had in reality been read into the text. The nineteenth century had superimposed its understanding of history upon Mark.

The viewpoint of Albert Schweitzer[2] was both an alternative to and a confirmation of the position of Wrede. Schweitzer agreed with Wrede that the Marcan narrative is not built upon historical considerations of a psychological, pragmatic nature. But instead of attributing this departure from normal history to the evangelist, Schweitzer attributed it to Jesus himself. Jesus was neither psychologically predictable nor pragmatically motivated, but rather was under the sway of a dogmatic, eschatological compulsion, and consequently lived a very unusual and unlikely life. Thus, by destroying the simple, understandable Jesus, Schweitzer implicitly weakened the case for the historicizing interpretation of the Gospels which he himself employed. For by tracing the eschatological element of the narrative back to Jesus himself, he eliminated from the history of early Christianity the necessity for any period when Jesus was 'still' looked upon from an objective, immanent point of view.

Further impetus in the new orientation was provided by Wellhausen's *Einleitung in die drei ersten Evangelien*, 1905. Wellhausen works

[1]Already in 1892 Martin Kähler had presented in *Der sogenannte historische Jesus und der geschichtliche, biblische Christus* the view that scholarship cannot get behind the Gospels to the 'historical Jesus', since the Gospels are not historical 'sources', but rather *kerygmatic* 'witnesses'. But Kähler's influence was felt only later.

[2]Expressed first in 1901 in *The Mystery of the Kingdom of God*, then in 1906 in *The Quest of the Historical Jesus* (esp. 328 ff.).

in general independence of Wrede and Schweitzer, and yet his conclusions tend to strengthen their consensus, as well as to point the new orientation in the direction of form criticism.[1] He clearly says of Mark (43) that 'the characteristics of real historiography [*Historie*] are lacking'. Mark does not write *de vita et moribus Jesus*. He does not intend to make Jesus' person comprehensible; rather Jesus' person has been taken up and dissolved (*aufgegangen*) in his divine calling, for Mark desires to present Jesus as the Christ (44). Mark's Gospel does not give the impression of being based on the reports of Jesus' intimates; instead, long circulation as oral tradition has given the material an 'uncomfortably drastic formation' (45). In one section of Mark, between Peter's confession and Passion week, there occurs a time shift from the life of Jesus to the life of the Church; here we are confronted with what is spoken by 'the Christ to Christians' (72). This section does not supply information as to the historical Jesus; rather: 'All these things are noteworthy signs of the times in which he [sc. the Marcan Jesus] places himself', i.e., the time of the Church (70–72). Mark is thus a combination of 'memoirs and gospel' (167).

C. RESULTANT CONFUSION: MARK AS MYTHOLOGY

The new tack in the interpretation of Mark rejected so completely the accepted canons of Marcan interpretation that the way stood open for a series of unlikely hypotheses, whose primary strength lay in the fact that they did not historicize Mark. W. Erbt, *Das Markusevangelium*, 1911, presented an interpretation of Mark in terms of astral mythology. In 1921 Arthur Drews renewed his attack upon the historicity of Jesus with a monograph *Das Markusevangelium als Zeugnis gegen die Geschichtlichkeit Jesu*, in which he drew attention to the 'mythological' point of view from which Mark was written. Old Babylonian traditions, together with astrological speculations, had been taken over by Jewish gnostics to construct a concept of a dying and rising Messiah. A similar interpretation was offered in 1924 by Hermann Raschke, *Die Werkstatt des Markusevangelisten*. The Marcan stories are but allegories of proper names venerated by the nascent religion. Raschke sees Mark as

[1]Cf., e.g., 45 of Wellhausen's work. (Citation is according to the second edition of 1911.) Cf. also Bultmann's evaluation of Wellhausen in 'The New Approach to the Synoptic Problem', *The Journal of Religion*, VI (1926), 341.

dominated by docetic and gnostic points of view, so that he arrives at the conclusion that Mark is the Gospel created by Marcion.

A scarcely needed refutation of the theses of these works was partially provided, more by coincidence than intention, by the publication in 1923 of Martin Werner's *Der Einfluss paulinischer Theologie im Markusevangelium*. This study was devoted to the disproof of any specific Pauline influence in Mark. Such an influence had been largely assumed on the basis of Gustav Volkmar's *Die Evangelien; oder Marcus und die Synopsis der kanonischen und ausserkanonischen Evangelien*, 1870. Werner showed that the assumed Paulinisms of Mark were doctrines widespread in early Christianity, while the specific Pauline concepts are largely lacking in Mark. Furthermore he displayed the inadequacies of Volkmar's symbolic and allegorical interpretations, which had provided the basis for the hypotheses of the mythological school. Thus Werner closed the door through which the anti-historical Marcan interpretation was moving into gnosticism, docetism, and mysticism.

The popularization of Wrede's thesis in England[1] by R. H. Lightfoot in *History and Interpretation in the Gospels*, the Bampton Lectures of 1934, has produced a similar group of unsuccessful attempts to achieve a positive centre from which to interpret Mark. Lightfoot himself shifted his centre of interpretation a few years later[2] from the messianic secret to Lohmeyer's geographic orientation.[3] This view has found some limited acceptance, but it suffers from inner contradictions and a lack of sufficient evidence.[4] Original Anglo-Saxon presentations based upon the new orientation are to be found in Philip Carrington's *The Primitive*

---

[1]Lightfoot's rôle in England as a transmitter of German research has been filled in America by Frederick C. Grant, who presents in *The Earliest Gospel*, 1943, the theses, e.g., of Wrede, Werner and Lohmeyer. The ground had been prepared for Lightfoot's and Grant's monographs by A. E. J. Rawlinson's Westminster Commentary of 1925.

[2]In *Locality and Doctrine in the Gospels*.

[3]Presented in *Galiläa und Jerusalem*, 1936.

[4]Cf. the limited acceptance of W. G. Kümmel in his review of Lohmeyer's book, *TLZ*, LXII (1937), 304–7, repeated substantially in 'Das Urchristentum', *TR*, n.F., XVII (1948–9), 16–19, and the criticisms of Albrecht Oepke, *Das neue Gottesvolk*, 1950, 183–7, and Rudolf Bultmann, *Theology of the New Testament*, I, 52, 56 f. Lightfoot himself in his last work on Mark, *The Gospel Message of St. Mark*, 1950, orientates himself more to the problem of history (see below).

Christian Calendar; a Study in the Making of the Marcan Gospel, and Austin Farrer's *A Study in St. Mark*, both of which appeared in 1952. Archbishop Carrington presents the gnosticizing symbolism characteristic of the German works, but within the framework of the cultic life of the Church. This is combined with Lohmeyer's geographic theory and the 'numbers' symbolism of the German mythological treatments. Farrer concentrates upon the latter trait, discovering complicated cycles and epicycles hardly discernible even to the initiated eye.[1] The basic weakness of these works is the same methodological error which Wrede detected in the Marcan research of the nineteenth century: the argument is not built upon what Mark clearly and repeatedly has to say, but upon inferences as to the basis of the Marcan order, a subject upon which Mark is silent.

The basic insight of the new orientation in Marcan research is that Mark was not an objective historian, but rather wrote from the point of view of Christian faith. This insight has proved to be ambiguous and subject to misleading inferences. The various treatments based upon the new orientation have seemed to understand 'Christian faith', in reaction to the historicism of the nineteenth century, as some mystic, cultic, gnostic religiosity, which more by accident than intention expresses its religious experience in terms of the action of a historical personage. These eccentric monographs on Mark have failed to recognize the basic fact that Mark finds meaning and divine action in history, and therefore intends to be recording history.

D. THE CONTEMPORARY TREND: MARK AS THEO-LOGICALLY UNDERSTOOD HISTORY

The most fruitful continuation of the new orientation consisted in form criticism, which was less concerned with the viewpoints of the Gospel authors (redactors?) than with the individual units within the Gospels. However, the Marcan material provided the point of departure for form critical studies, so that inferences with regard to Mark became apparent. Karl Ludwig Schmidt's investigation of the chronological and geographical framework of the Gospels[2] showed that Mark

---

[1]Cf. his retractions and corrections in: 'Loaves and Thousands', *JTS*, n.s., IV (1953), 1–14; and *St. Matthew and St. Mark*, 1954.
[2]*Der Rahmen der Geschichte Jesu*, 1919.

does not display a historian's concern for the externals of the history he is recording. On the other hand, form criticism eliminated pre-Marcan literary sources and Gospels. This accentuated Mark's rôle as 'historicizer' of material which had previously circulated in the context of the Church's life, but now appeared in the context of a presentation of Jesus.[1]

The intention of Mark to 'historicize' the oral tradition was traced to its origin in the centre of early Christian theology by Julius Schniewind.[2] The worship of the heavenly Lord is not a mystic experience separate from history, but is rather an awareness of living in a 'time of salvation', which would not be possible if the heavenly Lord had not brought that 'time' into history. The *kerygma* is the witness to the fact that the 'time of salvation' is present because the Messiah has been in history. To tell his 'history' as the inaguration of the 'time of salvation' is to witness to the present experience of the 'time of salvation'. The unity of the heavenly Lord of Mark's Church and the earthly Jesus of A.D. 30 lies in the continuity of the 'time of salvation'. The 'messianic secret' is but an expression of an understanding of history which embraces both the history of Jesus and the history of the Church. Since the Church sees its history founded in Jesus' history, it can witness to and explain its religious experience better by writing the history of Jesus as the Messiah than by describing its own religious life.

Schniewind's position is presented partially in terms of an interpretation of K. L. Schmidt's intention, and Schmidt accepts this interpretation as 'the best'.[3] Schmidt then defines the two limits between which a correct interpretation lies. One must avoid both an 'individualistic-psychological' approach, which bases itself upon a correct observation of the 'concrete-human' aspect of the Gospel narrative (Ebionitism),

---

[1]This emphasis in Martin Dibelius' *Formgeschichte des Evangeliums,* 1919, 2nd ed. 1933, is obscured in the English translation *From Tradition to Gospel.* Dibelius refers three times to Mark as 'historicizing' (*historisieren*) the material, but in only one case, p. 223, does the English translation preserve this significant term. In the other two instances it is obscured by the very free renderings: 224, 'would-be history'; 225, 'touched . . . up'.

[2]In his article 'Zur Synoptiker-Exegese', TR, n.F., II (1930), 129–89. The results of this analysis were applied in his commentaries to Mark (1933, 6th ed. 1952) and Matthew (1936, 6th ed. 1953) in the series *Das Neue Testament Deutsch.*

[3]In a lecture of 1933–4 on 'Das Christuszeugnis der synoptischen Evangelien', published in Beiheft 2 of *Evangelische Theologie,* 7–33.

and a 'collectivistic-cultic' or 'mythological' approach, which bases
itself upon a correct observation of those aspects of the Gospel which
cannot be grasped psychologically (Docetism). Although the synoptic
Gospels are not interested in uncommitted objective narration, they do
intend to narrate history. It is true that extraneous traits, such as debates
in the early Church's life or Hellenistic religious motifs, are visible in
the Gospel narration. Yet they are not told as the Church's religious
experience or as comparative religion, but are told as part of the history
of the Messiah. Therefore a 'messianic' interpretation should supersede
a 'stylistic' or 'comparative religion' analysis.[1] Here Schmidt has laid
bare the ambiguity involved in the simple affirmation of the new
orientation that the Gospels are to be interpreted primarily as a docu-
mentation of the history of the early Church. He himself operates upon
the basis of this new orientation, but proceeds to point to the fact about
the history of the early Church which had been largely ignored: the
early Church had a vital concern for the redemptive history of Jesus.
With regard to the affirmation *Deus dixit* the particular rôle of the
synoptic Gospels is to emphasize that this perfect tense, while being a
present perfect, is nevertheless a perfect tense.[2]

The most significant monograph on Mark in this period is that by
Hans Jürgen Ebeling, *Das Messiasgeheimnis und die Botschaft des Marcus-
Evangelisten*, 1939. This work presents first a history of the problem of
the messianic secret, in which the method of Wrede but not his solution
is defended. The second half of the work consists in retracing Wrede's
investigation of the silencing of the demons, the disciples' lack of
understanding, and the parable theory. The two motifs of secrecy and
misunderstanding reveal the Church's understanding of itself corre-
lative to its understanding of Jesus. These two motifs give expression
to the two sides of 'Christian faith's understanding of itself' (223). The
secrecy passages accentuate the majesty of Jesus so as to convey that
motif of faith which Ebeling designates 'the "must" of faith as the flow-

[1]Schmidt's illustration: Bultmann's interpretation of the temple-tax peri-
cope: 'Discussions of the Palestinian Church about responsibility for the
temple-tax', is less appropriate to the Gospel's intention than Calvin's: 'We
must attend, first of all, to the design (scopus) of this narrative; which is,
that Christ, by paying tribute of his own accord, declared his subjection, as
he had taken upon him the form of a servant.'
[2]The view of Schmidt is adopted by E. Käsemann in his lecture to 'old
Marburgers' in 1953, published in the *ZTK*, LI (1954), 125-53.

ing, free impulse of the heart.' Similarly the misunderstanding motif points to the revelation-character of Jesus in order to express the believer's tension and difficulty in arriving at a true understanding of himself.

Here for the first time in Marcan interpretation a concerted effort is made to characterize the religious experience of the Marcan Church as reflected in its presentation of the history of Jesus. Such an analysis is indispensable if Mark is to be seen as *kerygmatic* history in distinction from objective history. Yet the emphasis of Ebeling again jeopardizes the basic relevance of the fact that Mark presents his confession as a history not of himself but of Jesus. Ebeling does not look upon the Marcan Jesus as sufficiently concrete, real, or literal to be himself the subject of analysis and clarification. Rather each trait is immediately introverted into its existential meaning. The Marcan unity is sought in an understanding of religious experience, rather than in an understanding of Jesus as the basis of that experience. Marcan theology reflects a religious *a priori*, rather than a prior historical event. Thus Ebeling does not grasp the relationship between the history of Jesus as the inauguration of the eschatological 'time of salvation', and the existence of Mark as existence within this eschatological history. He reduces this relationship to the subjective tension in the believer's religious experience, thus neglecting the historical cast of Mark's presentation and the problem of history which it presents.[1] However it is only by defining Mark's understanding of history that a centre of interpretation can be located which does justice both to Mark's history of Jesus and to Mark's religious experience. Until this understanding of history is clarified, Marcan interpretation must fluctuate between the dissolution of the Marcan history of Jesus into Mark's religious experience, and the petrifaction of the Marcan *kerygma* into objective historiography.

E. THE CONTEMPORARY DEBATE ABOUT HISTORY

Ever since Kierkegaard's 'infinite qualitative difference' between time and eternity was introduced as the basis for theological thought,[2] and the reaction against 'historicism' became generally prevalent in

---

[1]Cf. the critical reviews by Lohmeyer, *TLZ*, LXV (1940), 18–22, and by Kümmel, 'Das Messiasgeheimnis im Markusevangelium', *Kirchenblatt für die reformierte Schweiz,* XCVI (1940), 2–5.
[2]Cf. the preface to the second edition (1921) of Karl Barth's *Romans*.

theological circles,[1] the relationship of Christianity to history has been central in theological debate. It is today becoming apparent that Barth's anti-historicism of the twenties was embedded in a positive concern for the meaning of history, which had been more apparent in the first (untranslated) edition of the *Römerbrief* (1919), and which has reappeared in the more recent volumes of the *Kirchliche Dogmatik*.[2] The sharp terminological cleavage between history and God which characterized the twenties has continued into the New Testament scholarship of the present primarily in the publications of Rudolf Bultmann[3] and Ernst Fuchs.[4]

It has become customary in German theology to distinguish between history in *bonam partem* as *Geschichte* and history *in malam partem* as *Historie*. The former refers to history as encountered existentially for the meaning it conveys, while the latter refers to history examined objectively for its mere factuality. But in Bultmann's writing *Geschichte* also tends increasingly to be used *in malam partem* for it occurs in such associations as 'inner-historical development', 'empirical-historical', 'national history', 'this-worldly history'. This kind of history can be prophecy or 'saving history' only by failing, coming to an end, i.e., by demonstrating the futility of trusting in man and thereby pointing to God, the *eschaton*.[5] Therefore, while Bultmann can still speak of 'God's

[1]Cf. Troeltsch's *Der Historismus und seine Probleme*, 1922, and his English lectures: *Christian Thought: its History and Application*, 1923.

[2]Cf. IV. i (1953), 246–50 for his specific appropriation of the attitude toward the synoptics characteristic of Schmidt and Käsemann.

[3]Cf. especially: 'Heilsgeschichte und Geschichte', *TLZ*, LXXIII (1948), 659–66; 'Weissagung und Erfüllung', *ZTK*- XLVII (1950), 360–83; and most recently his presidential address to the *Studiorum Novi Testamenti Societas* published *NTS*, I (1954), 5–16: 'History and Eschatology in the New Testament'. In the present discussion these essays are cited according to page number only.

[4]Cf. his lecture 'Christus das Ende der Geschichte', *Evangelische Theologie*, Jahrgang 1948–9 (1949), 447–61. He defines history (457, n. 18) as 'temporally fallen Being, in which man bequeaths his efforts at being able to live, since he attempts to surpass himself'.

[5]This is the argument in 'Weissagung und Erfüllung', 380 f. Similarly in 'Heilsgeschichte und Geschichte', col. 665 : 'According to primitive Christian thinking, Christ is rather *the end of history and of saving history*. The appearance of Jesus "as the time was full" (Gal. 4.4), signifies the eschatological event which places an end to the old aeon. From now on there can be no more history, and also no saving history, which precisely has reached in him its goal.' This is worked out more fully in 'History and Eschatology in the New Testament.'

deed in history',[1] he tends to give expression to the positive residue in the term 'history' by making use of two derivatives: 'saving event'[2] on the one hand and the 'historicity'[3] of human Being on the other. The former stands over against a linear, causally-connected, evolutionistic view of history, and accentuates the punctiliar, vertical aspect of the encounter with the *kerygma*. Such an encounter is 'eschatological', a term which now stands in antithesis to 'historical'.[4] The second term, 'historicity', does not characterize that which is encountered, but rather the attitude of him who enters the encounter. As such, it is a definition of 'faith', which is for Bultmann the pre-requisite to a definition of the 'ground of faith', and thus of normative Christian proclamation.[5] Both terms stand over against any objective view of history in its pastness and empiricalness, and indicate that history's meaning is apparent only as it happens and is encountered. They are also intended to avoid any group concept of history in favour of an individual relation to God, and to avoid any immanent, available and controllable relation to God.

Within the correlation between 'eschatological event' and 'historicity' is to be found the norm of Bultmann's theology.[6] The 'eschatological event' is the encounter with the message of the opportunity, the freedom,

---

[1]Weissagung und Erfüllung', 376. Cf. 'History and Eschatology in the New Testament', 16: 'The eschatological event has happened within history'.

[2]*'Heilsgeschechen.'* Cf. how this term is introduced into the article 'Heilsgeschichte und Geschichte', coll. 662ff., in working out the legitimate meaning of *Heilsgeschichte*, which term is then rejected. Similarly in the *Theology of the New Testament*, II, 121, the traditional terminology for expressing the Christian dialectic, history of salvation and world history, is replaced by the terminology 'revelation and history'. Here the term 'history' (*Geschichte!*) is reserved for the negative usage, and such an expression as 'historical revelation' becomes impossible.

[3]*Geschichtlichkeit*. Cf. 'History and Eschatology in the New Testament', 13. Is this also the German original of 'the history of man as person' (16)? A synonym is 'the temporality of Christian Being', cf. 'Heilsgeschichte und Geschichte', col. 666.

[4]This is supported by the non-historical dimensions of apolcalypticism's concept of the new aeon, which for the NT—at least its normative parts—is applied to the present existence of the Christian. This thesis is worked out in the essay 'History and Eschatology in the New Testament', with the conclusion (13 and 16): 'History is swallowed up in eschatology.'

[5]'Heilsgeschichte und Geschichte', col. 662.

[6]'Such an approach provides a more direct entry into the centre of the Bultmannian theology than does the ontological dualism postulated by Heinrich Ott in his valuable study of *Geschichte und Heilsgeschichte in der Theologie Rudolf Bultmanns*, 1955.

to be found in accepting one's death. (This message is the message
of 'the resurrection' or the *kerygma*.) But a message whose content was
a doctrine either to be accepted without insight or to be understood as
a demonstrable universal principle would provide an inner contradic-
tion to the existential meaning of the eschatological event itself. Such
a message would not lead to insight into one's historicity, but rather
the contrary. For 'historicity' means an attitude built upon the acceptance of one's individual death ('dying with Christ'), and therefore
directed toward the particular experiences of one's own life as the
scope of ultimate meaning for the individual ('risen with Christ').
Therefore the *kerygma* must proclaim that God is encountered within
one's historical existence. It is in this carefully defined context that a
'historical' encounter is for Bultmann indispensable. But such a context does not necessitate a history of Jesus. It is therefore questionable
for Bultmann whether the early Christian understanding of history
motivated Mark to begin the writing of Gospels, or whether the
synoptic evangelists have not already forsaken the original Christian
viewpoint.[1]

Bultmann's purification of the concept of history has become a norm
by which the New Testament literature is classified, with a scale which
runs from 'dehistoricizing' (Paul)[2] to 'historiography' (Luke).[3] In view

[1]The latter is suggested in vol. II of Bultmann's *Theology of the New Testament* (1955), by the rather cursory treatment of the synoptics within 'the
development toward the Ancient Church', after the New Testament has
reached its normative climax in John.

[2]*Entgeschichtlichung.* This identification is made and this viewpoint advocated by Bultmann in 'History and Eschatology in the New Testament', and
by Fuchs in 'Christus das Ende der Geschichte'. The core of their argument
(Bultmann, 132; Fuchs, 454) is based on the assumption that what Paul says
of the law in Rom. 10.4, can be generalized to apply to his concept of history
as well. Inconsistently enough, the term 'dehistoricizing' is also used by Bultmann in *malam partem* (*Das Urchristentum im Rahmen der antiken Religionen,*
1949, 65), to characterize Jewish legalism's neglect of responsibility for present history and its decisions, i.e., for the abandonment of its own historicity.
On 87 f. the positive usage of the term is distinguished as equivalent to 'de-
secularizing' (*Entweltlichung*). This means the rejection of all worldly security,
or of all that is at one's disposal, and the confrontation with one's neighbour
and with God's claim.

[3]*Historie.* The present depreciation of Luke stems from Franz Overbeck
(*Christentum und Kultur,* 1919, 80–82), who maintained the incompatibility of
history and Christianity. His position was thus diametrically opposed to that
of Harnack, who attempted to identify history and Christianity, and conse-

of this new 'tendency criticism', the relevance of investigating Mark's understanding of history is apparent.[1] For it is in terms of such individual analyses that the relationships within the New Testament literature, the dominant stream within the New Testament, and the validity or limitations of such constructions become visible. The present monograph does not approach Mark's understanding of history primarily with questions preformed by the current alternatives; rather the attempt is made to follow in form as well as content the Marcan material itself. But when this has been done, the relation to the current debate will be apparent.

---

quently thought well of Luke and his 'great historical work' (*Luke the Physician,* 1). Therefore the ensuing reaction against Harnack brought with it a depreciation of Luke. At the time that Overbeck's antithesis between history and Christianity was gaining acceptance through the dialectic theologians (cf. Karl Barth's 'Unerledigte Anfragen an die heutige Theologie', 1920, *Ges. Vortr.* II, 1–25), Overbeck's evaluation of Luke was cited with approval by Karl Ludwig Schmidt ('Die Stellung der Evangelien in der allgemeinen Literaturgeschichte', *Gunkel-Festschrift,* II [1923], 132): 'Nothing is more characteristic of Luke's conception of the Gospel history, in so far as he looked upon it as the object of historical narration, than his idea of giving the *Gospel* an Acts of the Apostles as its continuation. This is a tactlessness of world-historical dimensions, the greatest excess of false viewpoint which Luke committed.' Cf. more recently Ernst Käsemann, 'Das Problem des historischen Jesus', *ZTK,* LI (1954), 138: 'If the problem of historiography is in the other Gospels a sub-problem within eschatology, in Luke eschatology has become a sub-problem within historiography.' Similarly Bultmann, 'Heilsgeschichte und Geschichte', col. 665; 'History and Eschatology in the New Testament', 7: 'In the New Testament (if we set aside Luke-Acts) the Old Testament view of history is preserved as well as the apocalyptic view, but in such a way that the apocalyptic view prevails.' This classification of Luke as falling outside of the central view of primitive Christianity is worked out more fully in Bultmann's *Theology of the New Testament,* II, Paragraphs 53–54, 111 ff. This thesis with regard to Luke has been presented in detail by Hans Conzelmann, *Die Mitte der Zeit,* 1954.

[1]In *Die Geschichte der synoptischen Tradition,* 2. Aufl., 1931, 374, Bultmann states that Mark is more mythical than Matthew and Luke. This same view is presented in his *Theology of the New Testament,* II, 124–6. In distinction from Matthew's Jewish pattern of prophecy and fulfilment, Mark sees Jesus' life in the Hellenistic pattern of an 'epiphany of the Son of God', so that one could speak of the *history* of Jesus only in quotation marks. Emphasizing miraculous events like the baptism and transfiguration, Mark sees in Jesus 'the miraculous manifestation of divine dealing in the cloak of earthly occurrence'. Yet Mark, by the very fact of giving his presentation 'the form of an historical presentation, a "life of Jesus",' reflects the early Christian

awareness that their revelation comes not in the pictures of ecstatic vision-
aries, nor by some unconfirmable myth, but 'by an historical figure, Jesus'.
But Bultmann does not go on to inquire as to whether this side of the early
Christian message found expression in various details within the Marcan
presentation. Such an investigation is reserved for Luke, where such details
are then characterized as evidence that Luke falls without the scope of
primitive Christianity. Such a pattern of argumentation would be more
compelling if it had been first demonstrated that such motifs were lacking in
Mark.

II

THE MARCAN INTRODUCTION: 1.1-13

A. THE FRAMEWORK OF THE INTRODUCTION

Mark does not confront us as a philosopher writing about a concept of history, but as a narrator of history. His understanding of history must be deduced from the way he goes about writing it. His subject matter is 'the good news about Jesus Christ'. Yet the first verse is concerned not simply with the definition of the subject matter, but also with the location of its 'beginning'. Here Mark is using what seems to have been a technical term employed by the early Church for defining the *kerygma* (Luke 23.5; Acts 10.37) and apostleship (Luke 1.2; Acts 1.22; John 15.27). It was adopted by all the evenagelists in their presentations: Matt. 4.17; Luke 3.22; 4.21; Acts 1.1; John 1.1; 2.11. In view of such a deliberate beginning, one is struck by the fact that Mark opens *in medias res*. He picks up the story of Jesus at a point in his adulthood, whereas he had at his disposal (cf. 6.3) information concerning Jesus' background which he does not here use. Yet on the other hand his point of departure is not really hasty, but somewhat leisurely: he does not even begin 'the good news about Jesus Christ' with the principal subject Jesus, but rather with John the Baptist. It is only with vv. 14-15, 'after John had been arrested', that Jesus' own ministry is introduced, summarized, and initiated. To understand Mark in his approach to history, we must first understand his deliberate point of departure. When this is clarified we will already be on the way to understand his choice of subject matter, his particular way of treating his subject matter, his reason for writing history at all, and the understanding of history which underlies the whole.

The narrative is delimited by the coming (v. 4) and going (v. 14) of John, so that the fulfilment is initiated within the framework of the ministry of John. To be sure vv. 9-13 form a transition from John to Jesus: Jesus' baptism by John and his temptation. Yet this section still belongs to the introduction orientated to John's ministry: The stylistic similarity between v. 9 (Jesus' baptism by John), and v. 5 (John's general baptism), tends to place the baptism of Jesus within the framework of John's ministry of baptism. The break at v. 14 is also more prominent stylistically than that at v. 9, since v. 14 provides a formal termination to John's ministry and a formal introduction to Jesus' ministry.[1]

Evidently two motifs are at work in Mark: a distinction of John's ministry from previous Judaism (1.1 ff.), and a distinction of Jesus' ministry from John's (1.14 ff.). Both motifs are sufficiently attested elsewhere in the New Testament to make it apparent that we have to do here with a topic of some theological importance for the early Church.[2] The former motif is attested in Acts 1.22, 'beginning from the baptism of John', for the meaning of 'beginning from . . .' seems to be: 'beginning with and including'.[3] If Acts 1.22 is thus co-ordinate with Mark 1.1 ff., then Acts 10.37, 'beginning with Galilee after the baptism which John preached', is more co-ordinate with Mark 1.14, 'after John was arrested' (so Luke 3.20 f.; cf. also Luke 23.5). Both motifs are evident in the collection of sayings about John in Matt. 11.9–14, and in Acts 13.24 f.; 19.3 f.

The impact of the early Church's concern with including or excluding John's ministry is less felt in the formation of Matthew, for here the interest in the infancy has priority. But Luke has succeeded in providing

---

[1]The earlier tendency to make a principal break after v. 8, as in the Westcott-Hort text still followed by Nestle, has largely given way to the view here represented. The unity of 1.1–13 has been a repeated emphasis of R. H. Lightfoot, *History and Interpretation in the Gospels*, 1935, 62 f.; *Locality and Doctrine in the Gospels*, 1938, 113 f.; *The Gospel Message of St. Mark*, 1950, 16 f. Cf. also Vincent Taylor, *The Gospel according to St. Mark*, 1952, 151; Erich Klostermann, *Das Markusevangelium* (HNT), 4. Aufl., 1950, 1; Julius Schiewind, *Das Evangelium nach Markus* (NTD), 6. Aufl., 1952, 42; Ernst Lohmeyer, *Das Evangelium des Markus* (Meyer), 11. Aufl., 1951, 9, and on 1.9–11.

[2]This observation was made in a general way as early as Carl Lachmann, 'De ordine narrationum in evangeliis synopticis', *TSK*, VIII (1835), 584: 'An primum quidem omnium evangelicarum narrationum principium dubitari non potest quin fuerit ab Iohanne baptista ductum: nam quae Mattheus et Lucas de Jesu pueritia referunt, ea satis adparet paucis narratoribus propria fuisse nec vulgo cognita.'

[3]This is the meaning of Luke 23.5; 24.47; cf. also Matt. 20.8; John 8.9 (cf. Blass-Debrunner, *Grammatik des neutestamentlichen Griechisch*, 8. Aufl., 1949–50, Par. 419, 3). Since neither Luke nor the earlier tradition presents the twelve as having been with Jesus from the baptism on, Acts 1.22 must be looked upon as evidence of some theological interest in 'beginning with John'.

an infancy narrative which maintains the temporal precedence of John within the Gospel, while in Luke 3.20 f. the ministry of John is excluded from the period of Jesus' public ministry by a *tour-de-force*. In Mark's case, the two foci of interest are presented in their simplest form. Jesus' ministry begins only 'after John was arrested' (1.14), yet the 'beginning of the good news about Jesus Christ' (1.1) is the ministry of John. Thus the ministry of John is set apart, as having a special preparatory significance for the ministry of Jesus, from Judaism on the one hand and from Jesus' ministry on the other.

It is striking that the 'beginning of the gospel' is announced in v. 1, but 'preaching the gospel' is mentioned only at the second introduction (vv. 14–15).[1] John preached a 'baptism of repentance for the remission of sins' (v. 4); Jesus preached 'the gospel' (v. 14). Are we to understand that the good news began to happen—in the baptism that John preached—before it began to be proclaimed as such?[2] This is not inherently impossible, so long as the good news is not conceived of as some abstract, non-historical truth which, by being eternal, has no beginning save the beginning equal to its discovery or proclamation.

[1] By failing to observe this second motif Hans Conzelmann, 'Zur Lukas-analyse', *ZTK*, IL (1952), 20, has set up a point of opposition between Mark and Luke which does not exist: 'only now [sc. Luke 3.19 f., i.e., after John] arises—in conscious opposition to Mark—the entity "gospel", the kingdom of God'. However it is precisely Mark who says (1.14 f.) that after John was imprisoned the gospel began to be preached and the kingdom to be announced. Furthermore, Luke also has the other emphasis of including John: cf. the infancy narrative; the great significance he places upon dating accurately in terms of world history the beginning of John's ministry (but not Jesus' ministry!); and Acts 1.22 (which Conzelmann [ibid.] incorrectly harmonizes with the Lucan passages beginning *after* John).

[2] It is unlikely that Mark envisaged the content of the 'gospel' in 1.14 f. in conformity with the general early Christian 'gospel' of the cross and resurrection. This improbability is evident from Wellhausen's harmonizing attempts, *Einleitung in die drei ersten Evangelien,* 2nd ed., 1911, 100. Recognizing that the content of the 'gospel' is here 'the time has been fulfilled and the reign of God has drawn near', he states that for the Jewish listeners the judgement is not *good* news and the future coming of the kingdom no news at all. He concludes that the allusions here to 'gospel' are 'Christian embellishments' which do not agree with the content of the gospel as here stated by Mark. Thus 'gospel' has here the same *kerygmatic* meaning as elsewhere in the early Church, at the expense of making Mark's presentation in 1.14 f. meaningless. E. G. Gulin, *Die Freude im N.T.,* 1932, I, 33, proposes the 'victories' of the inbreaking kingdom as the content of the 'gospel' in 1.14 f. But Mark has recorded only one victory: the temptation.

If the good news is basically occurrence, something which happens, then it can begin to happen before it is proclaimed to have begun.

It is further remarkable that the good news is introduced (v. 2) with a prophecy announcing what *will* happen: κατασκευάσει, whereas the good news as summarized on Jesus' lips (v. 15) consists in an announcement of what *has* happened: πεπλήρωται, ἤγγικεν. The future tense in the prophecy is normal, and is restrained by the present tense ἀποστέλλω. But the exclusive use of the perfect tense (v. 15) to announce the nearness of a future eschatological consummation is worthy of note. For even though we must understand ἤγγικεν to mean 'has drawn near' rather than 'has come',[1] it still refers to something having taken place: the times have shifted, the kingdom is now near because it has moved from a vague distance to a near position, a shift which has already taken place. When vv. 2–3 offer a prophecy, and v. 15 speaks of the 'time' having been 'fulfilled', are we not led by Mark to look in the intervening narrative (vv. 4–13) for an event of fulfilment?

B. JOHN THE BAPTIST AS THE PROPHESIED PREPARER, 1.2–8

The fact that the ministry of John is seen from the viewpoint of fulfilment is confirmed by an analysis of the Marcan presentation of John. This presentation is characterized by a remarkable correlation of prophecy (vv. 2–3) and history (vv. 4–8).

The prophecy is not presented 'objectively' in the sense of a historical-critical exegesis of the Old Testament. Rather the prophecy is composed—by Mark or a predecessor—by uniting two separate passages, each of which stated the meaning of what has taken place: the way has been prepared; compare v. 2: κατασκευάσει τὸν ὁδόν, with

---

[1]The contrary view of C. H. Dodd, *The Parables of the Kingdom*, 1935, was refuted by J. Y. Campbell, 'The kingdom of God has come', *ET*, XLVIII (1936–7), 91–94. Dodd's reply, 'The kingdom of God has come', *ET*, XLVIII (1936–7), 138–42, was further refuted by K. Clark, 'Realized Eschatology', *JBL*, LIX (1940), 367–74. The debate seems to have been won by Campbell and Clark. See most recently R. H. Fuller, *The Mission and Achievement of Jesus*, (*Studies in Biblical Theology*, No. 12), 1954, 20 ff.; R. Morgenthaler, *Kommendes Reich*, 1952, 35 ff.; W. G. Kümmel, *Verheissung und Erfüllung*, 2. Aufl., 1953, 13–18. The same debate occurred a century earlier between Oldhausen (the viewpoint of Dodd) and von Hofmann, cf. *Weissagung und Erfüllung*, II (1844), 68: 'The perfect tense ἤγγικεν does not say that the heavenly kingdom is already there, but only that it is near.'

v. 3: ἐτοιμάσατε τὸν ὁδόν. What is prophesied is a next-to-the-last stage, a 'messenger' who will 'prepare', a 'voice' calling for 'preparedness'.

Similarly the historical narration (vv. 4–8) is directly concerned only with John; he for whom John is the preparation is not named. The history of John is not noticeably concerned with 'objectivity' in the sense of easily identifiable sources, fulness of detail, logical consistency, or the disinterested attempt to narrate 'as it happened to happen'. Hardly in a strictly statistical sense did 'all' (v. 5) come out to John (but cf. 11.32; Luke 7.29), nor do we feel called upon either to locate a specific 'wilderness' (v. 4) which runs along the edge of the Jordan.[1] Rather the historical narrative is formed and trimmed by Mark so as to set forth its true meaning: John is the prophesied preparer. The 'wilderness' is to be located not so much in relation to the Jordan as in relation to the third line of the prophecy.[2] 'All' come (cf. Acts 13.24) so that his 'way' may be truly prepared; for only a national repentance, not individual penitents, would constitute the anticipated preparation.[3] Such repentance was based on divine sanction, so that it was sometimes conceived of as limited to a certain period.[4] The detailed description of John in v. 6 occurs not out of 'biographical' interest, but to document the fact of the prophesied preparer's 'wilderness' life. The description of him as ἐνδεδυμένος . . . ζώνην δερματίνην περὶ τὴν ὀσφὺν αὐτοῦ has the specific purpose of implying John to be the preparer, Elijah redivivus (cf. 9.13), who is described in II Kings 1.8 as ζώνην δερματίνην περιε ζωσμένος τὴν ὀσφὺν αὐτοῦ. Other information available to Mark concerning John (cf. 2.18; 11.32) is passed by as unrelated to the idea of fulfilment, while his suffering (6.14–29; 9.13) is reserved for the dividing line between John and Jesus (1.14).

One historical fact about John which was not evident in the prophecy was nevertheless too prominent to be excluded: the fact that he

---

[1]Cf. K. L. Schmidt, *Der Rahmen der Geschichte Jesu*, 21 f.

[2]The 'wilderness' is however an old part of the tradition (Matt. 11.7, 18 par.), whose historicity need not be put in question. Cf. M. Dibelius, *Die urchristliche Überlieferung von Johannes dem Täufer*, 1911, 9 ff., and C. H. Kraeling, *John the Baptist*, 1951, 10 ff.

[3]Cf. Strack-Billerbeck, *Kommentar zum Neuen Testament aus Talmud und Midrasch*, I, 162–5 to Matt. 4.17; further Lightfoot, *The Gospel Message of St. Mark*, 19.

[4]Cf. Windisch, *Der Hebräerbrief* (HNT), 2. Aufl., 1931, Exkurs to Heb. 6.8; further Lohmeyer, 'Die Versuchung Jesu', *ZST*, XIV (1937), 645.

baptized. Yet this fact too is brought into conformity with the pro-phecy. The baptism is presented as something 'proclaimed', putting it into the framework of the preparatory action of a 'messenger' or of a 'voice of one crying'. This preparatory significance of John's baptism is stressed (v. 8) by stating the relationship and contrast between the ministries of John and Jesus in terms of two kinds of baptism. For apart from this interest in placing John's baptism in a correct relation-ship to Jesus, it is not customary for Mark to present Jesus' activity from the point of view of a kind of baptism he administered.[1] Further-more it is those whom John has baptized who are to receive Jesus' baptism: 'I baptized you . . . but he will baptize you.' Thus in spite of the contrasts in the two baptisms, Jesus' activity is clearly built upon and even to a certain extent modelled after the baptism of John. The reality or efficacy of the preparatory work of John's baptism is demonstrated in the subsequent sub-section (vv. 9–13), where the baptism of Jesus by the Spirit (v. 10) is prepared for in his baptism by John (v. 9), and this baptism is presented in formal parallelism to John's general baptism (v. 5). The break-through which is dramatically presented in vv. 10 ff. is made along the 'way 'which John's baptism has 'prepared'.

The narrative in which the fulfilment of the prophecy is presented culminates in its turn with John's prophecy (vv. 7 f.). For just as the history of John is understood as flowing out of and in accordance with the plan of God proclaimed by Isaiah, the history of Jesus is given the focus of fulfilment by the prophecy of John. John's spoken prophecy is itself a commentary, an explication of the meaning of his actions. His prophecy conforms to the same formal pattern of predecessor and successor as did that of Isaiah, save that now the primary emphasis is upon him for whom John prepares, and only the secondary emphasis upon John.

C. THE COSMIC LANGUAGE OF THE BAPTISM AND
TEMPTATION, 1.9–12

In John's prophecy we find ourselves already projected into cosmic language, and this shift in terminology is the most striking formal difference between the narrative concerning Jesus during the time of

---

[1] 10.38–39 and 1.8 are not parallel in meaning for Mark, although they could have been for John or Jesus.

John (vv. 9–13), and the narrative concerning John's own ministry (vv. 4–8). John's ministry is certainly intended as God's history, the fulfilment of prophecy, the effecting of the forgiveness of sins, the preparation of the messianic age. Yet it cannot be unintentional that in vv. 4–8 we find only John and the crowds, John baptizing and crowds repenting, whereas in vv. 9–13 (as intimated in the prophecy vv. 7–8) we find the heavens splitting, the spirit descending like a dove, a voice from heaven, God's Son, the Spirit driving him into the wilderness, Satan tempting, with the wild beasts and ministering angels. The disappearance of all humans from the narrative after the act of baptism is accentuated by the address of the heavenly voice to Jesus rather than to the crowd or John. Jesus has his place in the human, historical language with which John and his followers are described, but also in the cosmic language of God versus Satan.

The specific purport of the various events following immediately upon Jesus' baptism can hardly be made clear by separate analysis of each individually. Only the total of the various motifs can provide an indication of what is intended. The language of Jewish hope was not homogeneous, nor does the fulfilment here any more than in vv. 4–8 correspond exactly to preconceived ideas. Yet the exceptional nature for Jewish thought of such events as here portrayed and their intimate eschatological associations in the Jewish tradition make it clear that together this cluster of cosmic events signifies for Mark a decisive occurrence in the realization of the eschatological hope.[1]

[1]Perhaps the most remarkable parallel to Mark's baptism and temptation narrative is the Testament of Levi 18, 5–12: 'The heavens shall exult in his days, and the earth shall be glad, and the clouds shall rejoice, and the angels of the glory of the presence of the Lord shall be glad in him. The heavens shall be opened, and from the temple of glory shall come upon him sanctification, with the Father's voice as from Abraham to Isaac. And the glory of the Most High shall be uttered over him, and the spirit of understanding and sanctification shall rest upon him. For he shall give the majesty of the Lord to His sons in truth for evermore; and there shall none succeed him for all generations for ever. And in his priesthood the gentiles shall be multiplied in knowledge upon the earth, and enlightened through the grace of the Lord: in his priesthood shall sin come to an end, and the lawless shall cease to do evil. And he shall open the gates of paradise, and shall remove the threatening sword against Adam. And he shall give to the saints to eat from the tree of life, and the spirit of holiness shall be on them. And Beliar shall be bound by him, and he shall give power to His children to tread upon the evil spirits.' Here all the cosmic language of Mark's presentation is either explicit or implicit.

The temptation narrative, just like the baptism narrative, contains various traits which serve more to point to the exceptional nature of what is happening than to give a clear interpretation of it. Of more significance than the individual traits of the temptation narrative is the fact that this narrative is combined with the baptism narrative at all. The Spirit, rather than separating Jesus from historical involvement with its ambiguity and cost, takes him directly into encounter with evil in the person of its cosmic head. Thus the shift noted above from historical to cosmic language has not entailed a shift from historical involvement to mysticism or 'otherworldliness'. It is rather the reverse, with the cosmic language only serving to accentuate the ultimate significance of the engagement. For Mark, just as for Rev. 12, the shift in the status of heaven signalling the arrival of God's kingdom (Mark 1.10), corresponds to a more intense involvement on earth (v. 12), due in Rev. 12.12 to the shortness of Satan's time (cf. also Dan. 12.1; Acts 2.33). Basic to apocalypticism is the conviction that when the consummation is near, victory will come only after intensified struggle. The inauguration of the kingdom in history is for the purpose of bringing to an end the 'present evil aeon' and introducing the 'coming aeon'. Therefore the kingdom's Spirit embodied in Jesus plunges into the encounter. An essential part of the eschatological hope is the overthrow of the devil.[1] Only in this sense can we understand the action of the Spirit in driving Jesus to the wilderness as depicted here, and the inclusion of the temptation narrative in Mark's introduction at all.

D. THE CENTRAL MEANING OF THE INTRODUCTION FOR MARK'S GOSPEL

The Marcan introduction seems to have the purpose of presenting the inauguration of eschatological history in the baptism and temptation of Jesus. A more specific definition of Mark's conception of this eschatological history can be gained by investigating those traits which occur both in John's prophecy and in the two-fold fulfilment in baptism and temptation. For it must be in terms of such common factors that the whole presentation in vv. 7–13 finds its organizing principle and its central meaning for Mark. Terminologically it is the 'Spirit' (vv. 8, 10,

---

[1]Cf. Messel, *Die Einheitlichkeit der jüdischen Eschatologie*, 1915, 171 ff.

12) which gives unity to the three sections.[1] Therefore a clarification of the significance of the 'Spirit' in the introduction will serve to indicate the approach of Mark to the history he has begun to narrate.

The point of departure for an adequate interpretation is the fact that the term Spirit had in the Old Testament and Judaism a strong accent upon the idea of power.[2] This connotation of power is still vivid in Mark's use of the term 'Spirit', as is clearly evident at 1.12; 3.29 f.[3] In both passages the 'Spirit' operates as power: in 1.12 the 'Spirit' 'drives' (ἐκβάλλειν) Jesus into the wilderness; and in 3.29 the 'Spirit' is identified as the power operative in Jesus' 'driving out' demons 3.22 f. (also ἐκβάλλειν).[4] This relation of the πνεῦμα to power serves to give unity to the prophecy of John concerning one who is 'stronger' and who also baptizes 'with the Holy Spirit'. The superior strength is due to the power of the 'Spirit'.

Although Jesus' strength is compared in the prophecy with John's, Mark does not mean that they are competitors one against another, but

[1] The accentuation of differences in the conception and rôle of the 'spirit' in these three passages—cf., e.g., Lohmeyer, *Comm.*—can apply only to the pre-Marcan meaning of the allusions. On the background of the general rarity of the term πνεῦμα in Mark and the formal and material proximity of the three occurrences in 1.8–12, this term must be conceived of from Mark's point of view as having the same basic meaning throughout the context, and consequently as providing a line of connexion—not disunity—for the passage.

[2] A clear example is Micah 3.8: 'But as for me, I am filled with power, with the Spirit of the Lord, and with justice and might . . .' A Jewish parallel contemporary with Mark is Josephus, Ant. 8.408: γνώσεσθε δ' εἴπερ ἐστὶν ἀληθὴς καὶ τοῦ θείου πνεύματος ἔχει τὴν δύναμιν. The nearness of the two concepts of spirit and power is also confirmed by their association in the following passages: Luke 1.17, where John the Baptist comes ἐν πνεύματι καὶ δυνάμει ᾿Ηλίου; Luke 4.14, where Jesus comes ἐν τῇ δυνάμει τοῦ πνεύματος; Acts 10.38 . . . ἔχρισεν αὐτὸν ὁ θεὸς πνεύματι ἁγίῳ καὶ δυνάμει; I Cor. 2.4 . . . ἐν ἀποδείξει πνεύματος καὶ δυνάμεως; Rom. 15.19 δύναμις πνεύματος; II Tim. 1.7, . . . πνεῦμα τῆς δυνάμεως Cf. the presentation by Grundmann, *Der Begriff der Kraft in der neutestamentlichen Gedankenwelt*, 1932, esp. 56.

[3] Cf. E. Schweizer, 'The Spirit of Power', *Interpretation*, VI (1952), 260, and in his forthcoming article on πνεῦμα in the *TWNT*, VI. He points (261 f.) to the fact that the prophecy of John is not understood by Mark as the apocalyptic judgement of wind (πνεῦμα) and fire (cf. Matt. and Luke), but rather is brought into conformity to the early Christian idea of the πνεῦμα as the power of God within the eschatological history, evident in Jesus and promised (Mark 13.11) to the Church.

[4] This is the normal Marcan term for exorcisms: performed by Jesus: 1.34; 7.26; by disciples: 3.15; 6.13; 9.18, 28, 38.

rather that Jesus' strength exceeds John's against the common foe. The greater strength prophesied by John and fulfilled at Jesus' baptism with the Spirit is demonstrated at the temptation. This relation of the designation 'strong' to the struggle with Satan finds its confirmation and nearest parallel in the exorcism debate, the only other place in Mark where the term 'strong' recurs. Satan is called (3.27) the 'strong one' against whom Jesus struggles, in language based on the prophecy of Isa. 49.24 ff.[1] Jesus is not here named 'stronger', but the fact that he binds and plunders the 'strong one' makes the fact of his superior strength evident. Therefore the same passage concerning exorcism where the power of the Spirit is evident (see above), also indicates that this power is used against the strong Satan. Thus is revealed the inherent connexion between these two passages, and between the ideas of 'strength' and 'Spirit'.

The fact that the terms 'stronger', 'Spirit', and 'Satan' at the centre of the prologue form a coherent meaning of eschatological struggle has been confirmed by the exorcism debate, where all three elements recur. Clearly the explanation of the exorcisms in 3.21–30 is a close parallel in its theological meaning to the Marcan introduction. The struggle which took place in the temptation continues in the exorcisms of the Marcan narrative,[2] and the single event of the temptation becomes in the exorcisms an extended history of redemptive significance. This fact is of some relevance for the discussion in a subsequent chapter of history after A.D. 30 in Mark. For once the saving action of Jesus over Satan is divided into a series of stories, it has lost its single-event character and is already on the way to becoming a history open to potential continuation within the Church.

In view of the close relation between the baptism-temptation unit and the exorcism debate, the question arises as to why the baptism and temptation are separated from the body of the narrative by the new beginning at 1.14–15. This trait lets the reader sense not only a continuity, but a discontinuity, and indicates that the introduction is not

[1]Cf. Otto, *The Kingdom of God and the Son of Man,* 100 ff.
[2]Lightfoot, *History and Interpretation in the Gospels,* 65, erroneously sees in the temptation the whole of the preliminary struggle with evil which apocalypticism expected just before the end. His error is due to the fact that he interprets 1.15 as 'realized eschatology', i.e., the kingdom has (already) 'come upon you', so that the struggle preceding the kingdom must be terminated prior to 1.15.

merely the first in a series, but also the foundation of the series. Although the succeeding episodes flow uninterruptedly from one to the other, they are together separated from the introduction. John had disappeared from the narrative much earlier, so that the desire to separate John from Jesus could have been met without reintroducing him for this purpose (1.14; cf. Luke) nor is this John-motif central in the new introduction. Therefore the question must be raised as to whether there is not some further facet in the early Christian understanding of Jesus' history which Mark expresses by this line of separation.

It has already been suggested that the announcement in 1.15: 'the time *has* been fulfilled and the kingdom of God *has* drawn near', provides a first commentary on the baptism-temptation unit. Since this announcement is presented thematically at the opening of the public ministry, it tends to define the baptism-temptation unit as the basis presupposed by—and in this sense set off from—the whole public ministry of Jesus. It has become clear that the baptism-temptation unit finds its closest parallel in the exorcism debate. Therefore it would seem consistent to see in 3.27 a further allusion, even more specific than that in 1.14 f., to the relation between the introduction and the public ministry: 'no one can enter the house of the strong one and plunder his goods, unless he first binds the strong one [introduction, esp. the temptation], and then he can plunder his house [narrative, esp. the exorcisms].'[1]

Such a two-fold time reference with regard to the eschatological attack upon evil spirits is documented in the Testament of Levi 18.12: 'And Beliar shall be bound [Mark: "first bind the strong one"] by him and he will give power to his children to tread upon the evil spirits.' The fact that such a two-fold construction of Jesus' activity prior to his

---

[1]This exegesis has been challenged by Klostermann (*Comm.*, 2nd. ed.), who identifies the σκευή with the exorcised demons rather than the freed humans, and thus identifies the act of binding with the act of exorcism. However, Grundmann (*Der Begriff der Kraft in der neutestamentlichen Gedankenwelt*, 49 f.) has shown on the basis of Isa. 49.25; Test. Levi 18.12; Test. Zeb. 9.8; Jub. 10.8; Luke 13.16, that the 'booty' is more likely to be the humans involved. Klostermann then (3rd and 4th ed.) conceded the point in principle, but continued to maintain his interpretation of Mark 3.27 as an exception. His remaining arguments have already been answered in the discussion above. The assumption of H.-D. Wendland, *Die Eschatologie des Reiches Gottes bei Jesus*, 1931, 49, that the 'binding' refers to exorcism and the 'plundering' to the *parousia*, is negated by the fact—which Wendland himself conceded—that the exorcisms are not causal presuppositions of the *parousia*.

passion was envisaged in the early Church is demonstrated by Acts 10.38, which could very well be a commentary on Mark 3.27: 'how God anointed Jesus of Nazareth with the Holy Spirit and with power; how he went about doing good and healing all that were oppressed by the devil, for God was with him'. In so far as Mark's presentation of Jesus' life conforms to Acts 10.38, his understanding of Jesus' history can be accurately called '*kerygmatic*' in the stricter sense of dependence upon the early sermon's outline.[1]

It is probable that both kinds of time reference in this motif of the *kerygma* are rooted in teachings of the historical Jesus. Present references have been identified as authentic by most scholars for some time; past references are less obvious, but may also be detected.[2] It is this old tradition of an inaugural action prior to the public ministry, making it possible and serving as its basis and theme, which finds expression in the Marcan introduction. This tradition points to the coming of the Spirit and an initial victory over Satan, which are also the constituent elements in the theological meaning of the Marcan introduction. In this initial encounter between the eschatological Spirit and the ruler of the present evil aeon, the kingdom of God draws near. This event marks the 'beginning' of the last hour and thus of the Christian history (1.1). The basis has been provided for the ministry of Jesus, which consists in proclaiming the new situation (1.15), and in carrying through the struggle against Satan in the power of the Spirit.

[1]C. H. Dodd, 'The Framework of the Gospel Narrative', *ET*, XLIII (1931–2), 396–400, and *The Apostolic Preaching*, 1936, 46–51 of 2nd ed. (1944), has drawn attention to the public ministry in the *kerygma* as the outline upon which Mark was written. But he has not done justice to the fact that the *kerygma* does not outline any succession or order of events in the Galilean ministry to support the supposedly *kerygmatic* outline he finds in the Marcan summaries. The reference in Acts 10.38 to 'doing good' and exorcizing is hardly intended as a chronological order, and if it were, it would not correspond to the Marcan presentation. However, the *kerygma* does distinguish the public ministry as a whole from the baptism with which it begins and the passion with which it ends.

[2]Cf. my article on 'Jesus' Understanding of History', *JBR*, XXIII (1955), 17–24, where such a past reference is traced in the eschatological parables of Jesus. Cf. also Luke 10.18; Matt. 11.11a, 12; 21.32; Mark 11.30, as well as the echoes of John's teachings in Jesus' sayings.

III

THE EXORCISM NARRATIVES

A. THE DIRECTION OF THE INVESTIGATION

The term 'cosmic language' refers to specific allusions by Mark to the cosmic forces which transcend historical immanence and yet participate in the history Mark records. The introduction to Mark has made it clear that Mark speaks in cosmic language of a struggle between the Spirit and Satan. In distinction to the mass scenes and human milieu which characterize the ministry of John the Baptist, Jesus was presented as solitary, addressed privately from heaven as if John the Baptist were no longer present, and then driven into the solitude of the wilderness for the temptation. Jesus' context is the cosmic language of the opened heavens, the voice of God, the Son of God, the Spirit, Satan, angels and beasts. When this aspect of the introduction is envisaged, the expectation could arise that the Marcan narrative to follow would be more myth than history. The movement from the Baptist's crowds to the wilderness could seem introductory to 'war in heaven', 'Michael and his angels fighting against the dragon' (Rev. 12.7 ff.). The exorcisms which have already been related to the introduction would then serve as the nearest rapprochement of a mythological narrative to historical events. The 'eschatological history' would hardly be history at all. Only when this alternative is clearly envisaged can one evaluate properly the actual state of the facts with regard to the cosmic language in Mark and the actual rôle of the exorcisms in the narrative. Cosmic language is rare in Mark, occurring primarily at decisive points of the narratives; the exorcisms, rather than being the nearest point of approach to history in a myth, are the points in a historical narrative where the transcendent meaning of that history is most clearly evident.

Mark's references in the exorcisms debate (3.22 ff.) to the action of the Spirit through Jesus or the action of Satan through the demoniac are only partially 'cosmic' in language. Therefore the key in which the

narration is set is somewhat more subdued. The exorcism stories themselves refer to 'demons 'and 'evil spirits', and to Jesus as 'Son of God'.
They are put into the context of the struggle between the Spirit and
Satan by the debate in 3.22 ff. Yet the exorcism stories nowhere allude
to the Spirit and Satan, nor are the other cosmic terms of the introduction to the Gospel encountered. Rather the exorcisms are in several
respects more historical in form of presentation. In distinction from
Satan at the temptation, the demons who encounter Jesus are never
disembodied, but are rather in possession of humans through whose
organs they speak. The historical cast of the exorcism stories is also
evident from the fact that the scenes are presented as public, not
esoteric, taking place in the synagogue (1.23, 39), or in a tumultuous
crowd (3.7–12; 1.32–34; 9.14–27), or in such a way as to draw public
attention (5.14–20; [9, 38]). Exorcism was often accompanied by preaching (1.39; 3.14 f.; [5.19 f.]; 6.13), or teaching (1.21–28), or healing (1.32–
34; 6.13; 3.10–11). When Mark carries the cosmic struggle from the
solitary encounter with Satan at the temptation into the historical
setting of the exorcism narratives, it is already evident that he
proposes to describe the cosmic struggle as taking place in historical
occurrence.

The struggles between the demoniacs and the Son of God are sufficiently historical in tone to serve as a bridge between the passages with
predominantly cosmic language and the narratives where the language
remains more completely within immanent categories of human debate
and conflict. The central position of the struggle with demoniacs serves
to show on the one hand that the cosmic-language passages have very
much to do with history and are really a form employed by Mark for
stating a theological understanding of history. On the other hand these
historical struggles with demoniacs provide a working hypothesis for
interpreting the debates with opponents: although cast in more immanent language, these debates are not intended as only immanent or
relativistic by Mark, but represent for him the same eschatological
struggle in history. The sharpness of the debates as a matter of life and
death for Jesus is simply a subdued form of expression for the cosmic
struggle taking place in them. This most historical form of expression
thus maintains the same sense of unreserved involvement expressed by
the cosmic language.

We have identified three levels of Marcan language, which could be summarized schematically as follows: the Spirit and Satan; the Son of God and demoniacs; Jesus and his opponents. The three-fold classification of Marcan language cannot be pressed, but does provide an avenue of approach into the Marcan material by means of which Mark's central understanding of history can be traced into the more immanently-phrased parts of the narrative.[1]

B. THE EXORCISMS AS A DUALISTIC COSMIC STRUGGLE

The exorcisms are interpreted in 3.22–30 in terms of the cosmic struggle between the Spirit and Satan begun in the temptation. The exorcism narratives themselves do not refer specifically to the Spirit and Satan. But they reveal the presence of the same struggle by the sharply hostile and antithetic form in which the stories are presented. For at one important point the exorcism narratives differ from modern historical style: they do not presuppose the ultimate ambiguity or relativity of historical occurrence.

The personages in the exorcism narratives are designated in such a way as to make clear their opposing rôles in the cosmic struggle. Mark describes the demoniac as a 'man with an unclean spirit' (1.23; 5.2), or a person who 'has' an 'unclean spirit' (7.25) or a 'dumb spirit' (9.17). For Mark, the diagnosis consists simply in the presence of the demon, and he gives the fact of the demon a prominent place throughout his presentation.[2] The identifications of Jesus as 'Son ['holy one' 1.24] of God' (3.11; 5.7) also render the contrasting nature of the two antagonists evident. It is possible that the unusual term 'holy one of God' (1.24) is an allusion to Jesus as bearer of the 'Holy Spirit' (1.8) over

[1] A somewhat parallel procedure is followed by Wilhelm Wrede, *Das Messiasgeheimnis in den Evangelien*, 2, 7, when he bases his argument for a theological approach pervading Mark upon the accentuation of those passages which he regarded as the most 'unhistorical': the baptism, the resurrection of Jairus' daughter, the two miraculous feedings, Jesus walking on the water, the transfiguration, the angels with the women at the tomb. His argument is to the effect that a narrative including such incidents must be pervaded throughout by an attitude different from that of the objective historian, i.e., by a theological attitude. However, the present study differs from Wrede in that it does not ignore as irrelevant the historically-cast bulk of the narrative.

[2] Demon: 1.34, 39; 3.15, 22; 6.13; 7.26, 29, 30; 9.38; unclean spirit, in addition to the above: 1.26, 27; 3.11, 30; 5.8, 13; 6.7; 9.25; spirit: 9.20; dumb and deaf spirit: 9.25.

against the 'unclean spirit' (1.23, 26 f.).¹ Such a contrast between the two kinds of spirit is explicit in 3.29 f.

Jesus' refutation (3.22–30) of the scribal charge that he is possessed by Beelzebub serves to stop any confusion as to the nature of Jesus' super-human power, and concentrates the attention upon the contrast between the antagonists. All the demonic forces are united under Satan (vv. 23, 26). Any friendship to Jesus on their part is excluded by the reference to the fall of a divided kingdom (v. 24) or house (v. 25). Any friendship to the demons on the part of Jesus is excluded by the saying that a plunderer must first have bound the owner of the house (v. 27). Jesus' action is attributed to the Holy Spirit (v. 29). The rarity of this identification in Mark shows the importance the present issue has for him. This importance is also stressed by the designation of the scribal confusion as an unpardonable or eternal sin (v. 29).

The clear-cut antithesis between the personages in the exorcism narratives is accentuated by the hostile attitude in which their discussions take place. We do not find calm conversations, but shouts and orders. The demons 'shout' at Jesus: 1.23; 3.11; (5.5); 5.7; 9.26. In 5.7 the demon 'adjures' Jesus. Jesus 'orders' the demons (1.27; 9.25), or 'reproaches' them with an order (1.25; 3.12; 9.25). The only passage approaching normal conversation is in 5.9–13, after the struggle is over and the authoritative word of exorcism had been uttered (v. 8). This conversation does not serve to place Jesus and the demons in 'normal' relations, but rather to accentuate the completeness of Jesus' victory, a trait which recurs normally in the Marcan narratives. Jesus is not communing with the demon, he is disposing of him. The communion takes place with the liberated human (vv. 15 ff.).

The hostility which Mark expresses in his descriptions of the conversations is confirmed by an examination of what was said. Bauernfeind has shown² that the three sayings spoken by demons to Jesus (1.24; 3.11; 5.7) are all closely parallel to incantations of witchcraft in the magical papyri and elsewhere.³ Therefore the words could very well

---

¹Cf. Procksch, *TWNT*, I, 102. This interpretation is more probable than Lagrange's reference, *Évangile selon St. Marc,* 2nd ed., 1928, to the character of Jesus, or Taylor's reference to a content of Jesus' preaching which the demon had supposedly heard.

²*Die Worte der Dämonen in Markusevangelium,* 3 ff.

³Bauernfeind lists parallels to the οἶδά σε form (14f.) and of the σὺ εἶ form (21ff.) of address. The purpose is to get magical control of the person so addressed.

for Mark and his readers give the impression of a defensive magical incantation. This hostility is of course only accentuated by the reference in the demon's sayings to Jesus 'destroying' (1.24) or 'tormenting' (5.7) them, as well as by the opening challenge (1.24; 5.7): 'What have you to do with us?' In 5.7 the demon appeals to God against Jesus, in language commonly used *against* demons: ὁρκίζω σε τὸν θεόν.[1]

We should not be deterred from this hostile interpretation by the 'confession' that Jesus is the 'Holy One of God' (1.24), 'Son of God' (3.11), 'Son of the Most High God' (5.7). One may compare the 'confession' (12.13 f.) of the Pharisees and Herodians to Jesus as the ideal teacher, where their intention is specifically stated to be that of 'ensnaring' him. It is worthy of note that the 'confessions' of the demons are not limited to Jesus' title, but also reveal his rôle, 1.24: 'you have come to destroy us.' The statement does not refer simply to the coming of Jesus from Nazareth to the synagogue of Capernaum, but describes Jesus' coming to earth as a heavenly mission to destroy the demons, and thus reflects the cosmic scope of the struggle.[2] Here the loftiness of Jesus' person is seen not as an end in itself, but in its significance for the historical struggle in which he is involved. Similarly the other lofty designation of Jesus as 'Son of God' is not to be understood simply as an innocuous honorific title, but as a term with ominous implications for the demons. The term had been closely associated with Satan's opponent the Spirit in 1.10–12. Therefore the content of the demons' confessions reveals the impossibility of understanding these 'confessions' as friendly or reverent. Their purpose is rather to gain power over Jesus by using his secret, spirit-world name.

The fact that the demons kneel (5.6) and fall down (3.11) before Jesus does not eliminate the hostility of their intentions or render their 'confessions' devout. These gestures are recognition of the superior power of Jesus, and as such are servile. But they do not end the hostility of the demons, as the analysis of their words has shown. Rather the gesture provides the demons with the occasion for attempting to overcome Jesus' power by naming his name, or even by adjuring by God. Only when these attacks fail do they plead for the mercy which

---

[1]Deissmann, *Bible Studies*, 274 ff.
[2]Cf. similarly, 1.38; 2.17; 10.45 for the identification of various facets of Jesus' ministry as the purpose of his 'coming'.

their posture suggests (5.10–12), or perform a last act of defiance which reveals their real attitude (1.26).

The fact that Jesus silences[1] the demons' 'confessions' (1.25, 34; 3.11), and proceeds to cast them out (1.25; 5.8), confirms the inacceptability of their attitude. The act of exorcism is the characteristic attitude toward the demons mentioned with regard to Jesus: 1.34, 39; 3.22 f.; (7.26); (9.38); and his disciples: 3.15; 6.13; (9.18, 28, 38). Exorcism is specifically designated as 'plundering' in 3.27. The only reference in Mark to demon or unclean spirit which is not accompanied by an explicit exorcism is 3.11 f., where in a summary passage Jesus' command to be silent suffices. A further indication of Jesus' opposition is to be discerned in 9.38–40, where the disciples do not want to recognize as an ally a person casting out demons in Jesus' name, since the person is not an official disciple. Jesus, recognizing the existence of only two sides, reverses their decision and declares that such action proves the person in question to be on Jesus' side: 'No one who does wonders in my name is able soon to speak ill of me. For he who is not against us is for us.' Thus Jesus' attitude confirms the original accusation of the demons (1.24): 'You have come to destroy us.' Prior to the Marcan context, and apart from the commentary in 3.22 ff., the exorcism stories resembled many exorcism stories of the ancient world, and could have been understood in the same non-eschatological way (cf. Matt. 12.27 par.). In the Marcan presentation they depict a cosmic struggle in history to inaugurate the eschatological reign of God.

---

[1]Even Wrede, *Messiasgeheimnis*, 33, n. 1, concedes with regard to 1.25: 'Φιμώθητι does not in and of itself say that Jesus does not desire the messianic address; rather he simply strikes down the demon's self-assertion evident in his speech. In 4.39 Jesus says the same thing to the sea.' But then Wrede adds: 'Nevertheless the evangelist seems, in view of the parallels [!], to mean that Jesus by his reply also rejects the messianic address.' Cf. Bauernfeind, *Die Worte der Dämonen im Markusevangelium*, 31; Ebeling, *Messiasgeheimnis*, 128 ff.; 'Against the demonstrated intention of the demon . . .' Wrede (37), maintains that the reason for silencing demons cannot be their demonic nature, since this explanation would not apply to the silencings following the raising of Jairus' daughter (5.43) and the healing of the deaf-mute (7.36). But Wrede forces this parallel at the expense of ignoring the contrast between the hostility in the commands to demons and the absence of such hostility in the other cases. Furthermore the basic assumption of Wrede (36), that all the silencings in Mark must be understood in the same way, is open to serious question, in view of the variety in form and mood of the silencings.

C. THE OUTCOME OF THE EXORCISM STRUGGLES

The exorcism narratives have been seen to present a contrast between the personages of these scenes, which helped to identify in them the continuation of the cosmic struggle within history. However, there is a second contrast within the exorcism stories: that between the violence and destructiveness of the demon in the human he possesses, and the tranquillity and communion in the scenes of Jesus with the liberated person. An analysis of this contrast will make it evident that Mark's understanding of history not only includes the presence of the cosmic struggle, but also the presence at places within history of the victory and of the resultant idyllic status which follows upon that struggle and victory.

The actions of the demons are violent, directed toward injury and death. In 5.3–5 the demon's violence is such as to break all chains and foot bonds, and he cannot be tamed. The demoniac lives among tombs and mountains, crying out and bruising himself with stones. In 9.17, 25 the demon has rendered the boy deaf and dumb; it casts him down, causing him to foam, grind his teeth and become rigid (v. 18); it casts him into the fire and into water to destroy him (v. 22). The swine rush into the sea and are drowned (5.13), after the legion of demons enters them. This violence is only accentuated by the presence of Jesus. His command of exorcism produces convulsions and shouting (1.26; 9.26). At the sight of Jesus the demon convulses the epileptic boy, who, falling on the ground, rolls about foaming (9.20). After the exorcism the boy became like a corpse and the crowd took him for dead (9.26).

The close association of this violence to physical harm and death is relevant to Mark's understanding of the crucifixion and resurrection. The sudden reversal of the situation as the passion narrative is replaced by the Easter story is already anticipated in the exorcism stories, and here the shift is identified as due to the victory over the demon, i.e., Satan. Following upon the act of exorcism, the scene is depicted so as to make it evident that violence and death itself have been cast out. Jesus' cure of the epileptic boy is described in terms of resurrection: ὁ δὲ Ἰησοῦς κρατήσας τῆς χειρὸς αὐτοῦ ἤγειρεν αὐτόν, καὶ ἀνέστη, 9.27 (cf. also 5.41 f.). The contrast between the two states is also sharply drawn at the end of the story of the Gerasene demoniac, where (5.15) the liberated man is seen with Jesus 'seated, clothed, and in his right mind', and the remark is specifically made that this is 'he who had had Legion'. Jesus sends him back to his family to proclaim his liberation (5.19) whereas the demon had forced him to make his home among the tombs (vv. 2 f., 5).

In addition to the exorcisms, other miracle stories accentuate the contrast between the situation before and after the cure. It is appropriate to envisage these miracle stories of Mark as a continuation of the same struggle as that carried on in the exorcisms. Judaism normally attributed various kinds of disease and misfortune to the action of demons.[1] Furthermore there are traces of exorcism language in three of the other Marcan miracle stories: 1.43 καὶ ἐμβριμησάμενος αὐτῷ εὐθὺς ἐξέβαλεν αὐτόν; 4.39 ἐπετίμησεν τῷ ἀνέμῳ καὶ εἶπεν τῇ θαλάσσῃ σιώπα, πεφίμωσο; 7.35: καὶ εὐθὺς ἐλύθη ὁ δεσμὸς τῆς γλώσσης αὐτοῦ. The similarity in language to the exorcisms is evident from the fact that ἐκβάλλειν (1.43)[2] occurs of exorcisms in 1.34, 39; 3.15, 22f.; 6.13; 7.26; 9.18, 28; ἐπιτιμᾶν (4.39) occurs addressed to demons in 1.25; 3.12; 9.25;[3] φιμοῦν (4.39) occurs as the command to demons in 1.25; and δεῖν (7.35) occurs in 3.27 to describe Jesus' action making exorcism possible.[4]

In spite of the nearness of miracle stories to exorcisms, the hostile opposition which characterized the exorcism narratives is largely lacking from those miracle stories which are not specifically exorcisms.

[1]Cf. Foerster, *TWNT*, II, 13 f.

[2]Lohmeyer remarks that ἐκβάλλειν alone is not a technical expression for exorcism, and that the object αὐτόν refers to the leper, not a demon. This indicates that an exorcism is not intended in the Marcan text as it now stands. However in view of the varied conjectures as to textual corruptions and conflation of stories (Lohmeyer himself conjectures the latter!), attention needs to be called to the fact that the story of the leper contains a verse largely unintelligible in its present setting, but admirably suited to an exorcism narrative. Even on the basis of the text as it now stands, the anger of Jesus can only be explained in terms of his opposition to the combined forces of disease, death, sin, and Satan. Cf. Campbell Bonner, 'Traces of Thaumaturgic Technique in the Miracles', *Harvard Theological Review*, XX (1927), 171–81, and Kirsopp Lake, 'ΕΜΒΡΙΜΗΣΑΜΕΝΟΣ and 'ΟΡΓΙΣΘΕΙΣ, Mark 1.40–43', *HTR*, XIV (1923), 197–8.

[3]Cf. Stauffer, *TWNT*, II, 623.

[4]Further parallels from outside Mark tend to confirm this demonic association of the concept of 'binding' and 'loosing': e.g., Luke 13.16; Acts 20.22; Rev. 20.2. Cf. Büchsel, *TWNT*, II, 59 f.; Bauer, *Wörterbuch* on δεσμός, δέω; Str-B, I, 739. Further examples, esp. of binding the tongue, are given by Adolf Deissmann, *Light from the Ancient East*, 304–7.

Nevertheless Jesus' opposition to the disease is as much a matter of course as his opposition to the demons. It may be of some significance that the only specific references to hostility in the miracles seem to be in the healing of the leper and the stilling of the storm, two of the instances where the language approaches nearest to that of the exorcisms.

Although hostility is not prominent in the miracle stories, these stories share the other significant trait of exorcism narratives: a sharp contrast between the state before and after the action of Jesus. The compassion-arousing situation of 'the sheep not having a shepherd' combined with the lateness of the hour, the loneliness of the place, the limitation of funds, and the scarcity of food at hand (6.34–38), stands in sharp contrast to 'all' who 'eat and are filled' with much left over, in spite of the vast size of the crowd (6.42–44). In the second feeding there occurs the same emphasis upon a compassion-arousing crowd, which is three days without food and too feeble to reach distant homes without nourishment (8.1–3). One observes also the same deserted location of the scene and the same scarcity of food on hand (vv. 4. f.). This situation is also contrasted with the 'eating and being full', with much left over, in spite of the vast size of the crowd (vv. 8 f.). The amplitude of the food which remains is accentuated as the point of both stories by the discussion in 8.19–21.

In the 'great storm of wind', the waves beat into the boat, which fills with water, so that there is danger of perishing (4.37 f.). This stands in contrast with the winds ceasing and the 'great calm' of v. 39.

When the terminations of miracle stories are not monopolized by other such favourite motifs as the crowd's awe or the unrestrained testimony of the cured person, there is often a motif to accentuate the completeness of the cure: Peter's wife's mother resumes her rôle as hostess (1.31); the leper receives official priestly confirmation of his cure (1.44); the paralytic takes up his bed and walks (2.11 f.); the man with the withered hand stretches it out 'and it was restored' (3.5); the woman with the issue of blood goes 'in peace' and is 'healed of her disease' (5.34); Jairus' daughter eats food (5.43); the deaf mute has his hearing restored, the bond of his tongue is loosened, and he speaks 'correctly' (7.35); the blind man at first sees men as walking trees (8.24), but when Jesus completes the cure he sees everything 'clearly' (v. 25).

Such motifs are inevitable in miracle stories, and have many parallels in other literatures.[1] Yet in some of the scenes the accent upon the fact of a residuum following the action is so accentuated, as in the two feedings, as to surpass what is necessary to prove the fact of the miracle. Furthermore the fact that the cure has the spiritual significance of a restored communion is often accentuated, as in the motif of sending the cured person home (2.11; 5.19; 8.26), as well as the scene with the cured Gerasene demoniac. The outcomes of the cures do not consist in a dedication to the contemplative life outside the course of history, but rather in a restoration to society, a return from seclusion back into the historical process.

The analysis of the exorcisms and other miracle stories brings us to the point from which the remainder of Mark, where demons are not mentioned and the language seems correspondingly more historical, can be understood. Jesus' unrelenting opposition in the exorcism narrative ceases abruptly when the human and the demon are separated. The purpose of this antagonism becomes clear: Jesus is struggling for life and communion on behalf of the possessed person. Both of these characteristics of a true historical existence had been opposed by the demon. These scenes which are nearest to the cosmic scene of the baptism and temptation have not by this fact turned us away from history. Rather, they have served to present the understanding of history not only underlying the exorcisms, but, as we are subsequently to investigate, also the whole of Mark's narrative. For Mark, history is not ultimately ambiguous or relativistic; rather it has two clear-cut and irreconcilable alternatives in it, which can at times be stated as simply as Son of God *versus* demon, Holy Spirit *versus* unclean spirit. Because of this clear alternative in history, struggle between the two opposing objectives of life or death, communion or segregation, is understandable. Only if history offered no real alternatives and no real results would inaction, 'other-worldliness' and resignation be appropriate. It is Jesus' function to enter this struggle on behalf of the true destiny of mankind and with his heavenly power to carry through to the victory, and to the life and communion it brings.

[1]Cf. esp. Dibelius, *From Tradition to Gospel,* chap. IV, 'Tales', 70–103.

IV

FROM THE DEBATES TO THE
RESURRECTION

A. THE RELATION OF THE DEBATES TO THE EXORCISMS

It has become clear that the exorcisms are understood by Mark in terms of the cosmic struggle inaugurated at the baptism and temptation of Jesus. Thus a bridgehead has been established within the body of the Marcan narrative for the thesis that this historical narrative is itself envisaged in terms of that cosmic struggle. The validity of this thesis depends upon whether or not the remainder of the Marcan narrative material, when cosmic language and references to demons are lacking, is intended as a continuation of that cosmic struggle. It is in terms of this question that the discussion now turns to the debates within Mark. For they not only form an important segment of Marcan material, but are also closely related to the exorcisms on the one hand and to the remainder of the Marcan narrative on the other.

The debates have been subjected to formal analysis by the form critics. Most of them were treated among the 'paradigms' by Dibelius,[1] but a separate category of '*Streitgespräche*' (lit. 'conflict discussions', or 'disputes'), was identified by Albertz[2] and Bultmann.[3] The latter term is a more accurate designation of their original '*Sitz im Leben*', inasmuch as rabbinic parallels[4] make it evident that the form arose within the setting of public debate, not in the cultic atmosphere of the sermon for believers. The debates do lead to a significant saying of Jesus of illustrative ('paradigmatic') value; yet it is of equal relevance that this saying is the climax of a struggle. The truth of God is not given as didactic exposition, but as the result of conflict, attained through effort, and as evidence of a break-through in the attack against evil.[5] This is the case both in the debates with Jesus' opponents and in the

---

[1]*From Tradition to Gospel*, 37 ff.
[2]*Die synoptischen Streitgespräche*, 1921.
[3]*Die Geschichte der synoptischen Tradition*, 2. Aufl., 39 ff.
[4]Cf. Bultmann, 42 ff.
[5]Cf. Ebeling, *Messiasgeheimnis*, 55.

debates with his disciples. In this sense Bultmann's association of the *Streit-und Schulgespräche* is preferable to Albertz' exclusion of the debates with disciples. On the other hand Dibelius is right[1] in pointing out that some of the Marcan debates (3.22–30; 7.5–23; 10.2–12) do not present the same form as those designated '*Streitgespräche*', so that as a matter of fact there is no single form for the debates in Mark. The present discussion on the Marcan debates is not limited to those conforming to any one 'form', but embraces all the Marcan debates.

The *Streitgespräche* in their pre-Marcan oral form are similar to the rabbinic debates.[2] However Mark is not concerned to maintain this set form. This is particularly evident in the case of the debate about ceremonial cleanliness (7.1 ff.). Furthermore Mark envisages a basic distinction between Jesus' teaching and that of the rabbis (1.22: 'not as the scribes'). For Mark, the nearest parallel to Jesus' debates is not the rabbinic debate, but rather the exorcism. This is evident from the fact that he chooses an exorcism story in the synagogue (1.23 ff.) to illustrate Jesus' unusual synagogal teaching which has 'authority' (1.22). This encounter with the demon includes violent debate, so that its summary (1.27) not only repeats the 'authority' motif, but also repeats the concept of a 'new teaching'. Thus Mark provides the exorcism as the pattern for interpreting the debates in the synagogues.[3]

There is also a similarity of form between the exorcisms and the debates. The demon advances upon Jesus with a hostile challenge, only to be silenced by an authoritative word of Jesus (1.23–26; 3.11 f.). The debates with the Jewish authorities likewise begin normally with a hostile question or accusation of the opponent, which is frustrated by Jesus' definitive reply: 2.6–11; 2.16–17; 2.18–22; 2.24–28; 3.2–5; 7.5–15; 8.11–12; 12.18–27. Sometimes his reply consists in taking the initiative, which calls forth a further statement of the opposition before Jesus' final word: 10.2–9; 11.27–33; 12.13–17. The same phenomenon occurs in the exorcism of 5.6–13.[4] Jesus' initiative is also accentuated by those

[1]*From Tradition to Gospel,* 222.

[2]Cf. Bultmann, *Die Geschichte der synoptischen Tradition,* 2. Aufl., 42 ff.

[3]Dibelius, *From Tradition to Gospel,* 43, classifies 1.23 ff. among the 'less pure' paradigms, and thus associates this exorcism with the debates. Albertz, *Die Synoptischen Streitgespräche,* 152, recognized the association of the debates with the exorcisms.

[4]Cf. Albertz' summary of the form of the *Streitgespräche, Die Botschaft des Neuen Testaments,* I, 1 (1947), 67 f., which could equally well characterize the exorcisms.

scenes where the accusing question was addressed to the disciples but not to him (2.16), or where it was not spoken aloud at all (2.6 f.; 3.2), but is nevertheless drawn out and refuted by Jesus. A similar shift from the disciples to Jesus is present in the exorcism story of 9.14 ff. The discussions with disciples or 'neutrals' do not display such overt hostility as do the exorcisms; yet the rejection of a false understanding and the affirmation of a clearcut and definitively true understanding is maintained: 3.31–35; 6.2–4; 7.14–15, 17–23; 8.27–30, 31–33; 9.38–40; 10.13–16, 17–22, 35–45; 13.1–2; 14.3–9. Thus there is considerable formal similarity between the exorcisms and the debates. It would be an error to associate the exorcisms only with the miracles, as if the healing action were the only constitutive element in the exorcism. This would be an all too medical interpretation of the exorcisms, and to this extent a modernization. The exorcisms are also struggles of minds, or will, and consist in words, as well as action. They culminate in an authoritative saying, with which the issue is settled. All these are points of similarity to the debates.

It is true that the exorcisms are drawn into close association with the healings by the fact that diseases (and other natural evils such as storms) were associated with the action of demons, so that there is not too great a distinction between an exorcism and other miracles in Mark. But an examination of the debates in Mark makes it clear that there is also an intimate relationship of meaning between the exorcisms and the debates. Just as there are traces of exorcism language in the miracle stories,[1] there are equally clear indications in the debates that they too are the action of Satan. The debates with the Jewish authorities are designated 'temptations' (8.11; 10.2; 12.15), thus making their diabolic instigation clear. The debates with the disciples concerning the passion are put into this context by the pointed attribution of the disciples' attitude to Satan (8.33), and the designation of the danger to which they are exposed in view of the passion as 'temptation' (14.38).

The cosmic struggle has here reached a more subtle form and is stated in more immanent language than was the case in the exorcisms.

---

[1] The 'sigh' which in the miracle story (7.34) is an 'expression of collected strength' having parallels in the magical papyri (Bauer, *Wörterbuch*, 4. Aufl., on στενάζω), recurs in a debate with the Jewish authorities (8.12). Cf. C. Bonner, 'Traces of Thaumaturgic Technique in the Miracles', *HTR*, XX (1927), 171–81.

But just as was the case there, Mark is not concerned either with purely immanent temptations, nor with purely inward and mental temptations; rather the concept is of that of 'trials' instigated by Satan and consisting in a historical encounter in a specific situation.[1] It is therefore evident that Mark not only presents the debates in a form similar to that of the exorcisms, but also envisages the meaning of the debates in a way similar to the exorcisms. The debates are a continuation of the cosmic struggle initiated at the baptism and temptation and carried into the narrative of Jesus' public ministry first by the exorcisms.

B. THE TRUTH OF ESCHATOLOGICAL HISTORY IN THE DEBATES

The tendency of the debates with Jewish authorities is to attack the ambiguity of a historical situation whose truth is confused by the evil intentions of the opposition. Jesus reduces the confusion to clarity so as to reveal the truth inherent in the historical situation. Just as in the debate concerning exorcism, the affirmation of the truth of history is rooted in the affirmation of the presence of eschatology in history.

Both the break-through to the truth of history and its eschatological basis are apparent in the first group of Marcan debates (2.1–3.6). When Jesus forgives sin, he is charged with 'blasphemy,' for 'who is able to forgive sins except one, God?' (2.7). This confused interpretation is answered categorically (2.10): 'The Son of Man has authority to forgive sins on earth.' Here clarity is reached not in terms of a general principle, but rather in terms of the presence of the eschatological Son of Man in history. The confusing implication that 'eating with tax gatherers and sinners' means advocating sin, is clarified as the action of the 'doctor', who is 'calling' sinners (2.16 f.). The illustration of the doctor is not left as a general principle, but rather is focused on the 'coming' of Jesus. The accusation of impiety in not fasting is clarified by stating that the mournful significance of fasting is inappropriate during (eschatological) marriage celebrations (2.19). The antithesis is further clarified by the distinction between a 'patch of unshrunk cloth'

[1]Compare the Rabbinic understanding of Satan's tempting activity, Messel, *Die Einheitlichkeit der jüdischen Eschatologie*, 179. Illustrations are given by Weber, *System der altsynagogalen palästinischen Theologie*, 1880, 243. The gentile environment with its temptation to hellenize is an example of Satan's activity (Messel, 163 ff.).

and an 'old coat' (v. 21), and the distinction of 'new wine' from 'old skins' (v. 22). Thus the true conduct Jesus advocates is based upon the fact of a new situation, apart from which the old ways would still be valid. Even when the Church returns to the custom of fasting, the practice is reinterpreted eschatologically as a living memory of the bridegroom (v. 20). The problem of misconduct in plucking grain on the Sabbath is reduced to the clear alternative of the 'Sabbath made for man' over against 'man for the Sabbath' (2.27). But this anthropological definition of true Sabbath conduct is based on the creation intention of God, for the topic of discussion (2.27) is the purpose of God at the creation. The validity of that original purpose over against current practice is based upon the presence of the eschatological Lord of the Sabbath (2.28). The similar unclarity about 'healing on the Sabbath' (3.2) is reduced to the unambiguous alternatives of Sabbath conduct: 'do good or do evil', 'save life or kill' (3.4).[1] The reality of this distinction is then revealed in the hardness of heart of the Jewish leaders (3.5), within the sway of an evil age, and the freedom of Jesus, acting in terms of the eschatological reign of God. Thus the debates in 2.1–3.6 present an affirmation of real alternatives between right and wrong within history, and base this affirmation upon the reality of the *eschaton* within history.[2]

The subsequent debates reveal the same tendency to overcome the relativity and ambiguity of history, to set truth against error, and to champion this truth.[3]

Thus we have through a long series of debates a process of 'setting the record straight' with regard to truth, where Jesus is shown both as one who acts truly in history and one who clarifies truly the meaning of history. The eschatological basis of this understanding of history is not stated positively in these passages in terms of the nearness or dawning of God's reign.[4] However it is implicit in the negative treatment of

[1]These are the same alternatives encountered in the exorcisms; and just as 'having a withered hand' (vv. 1, 3) corresponds to 'having an unclean spirit', 'healing' (v. 2) corresponds to 'casting out', and the order 'Stretch out your hand' (v. 5) corresponds to the command 'Come out'.

[2]The eschatological orientation of the whole section (2.1–3.6) has been demonstrated by Joachim Jeremias, *Jesus als Weltvollender*, 21–32, and Harald Riesenfeld, *Jésus transfiguré*, Appendix III, 318–30.

[3]For an analysis of the antithetic structure of these debates, cf. my work *Das Geschichtsverständnis des Markus-Evangeliums*, 1956, 61 f.

[4]This point has been accentuated by Dibelius, *From Tradition to Gospel*, 222,

the Jewish tradition, which is secularized from a vantage point associated with God (7.1–23). We do not have to do with a Marcionite-like rejection of the Jewish God, but rather a rejection by the Jewish Messiah of the empirical Jewish tradition by appeal over Judaism's head to its God and scriptures. Therefore it is clear that here too the basis of argumentation is eschatological. The pattern of argumentation is to associate the Jewish authorities with the non-godly tradition of the present evil aeon, and to associate Jesus with the godly tradition of the holy history of the Old Testament, as its eschatological fulfilment. It is no accident that Jesus' allusions to Scripture tend in Mark to come from passages of 'pre-historical' intention (Eden) and 'post-historical' consummation, and from those points in the Old Testament where the divine meaning of Israel's history is particularly accentuated. With regard to divorce Jesus appeals over against legislation based upon the evil in history ('your hardness of heart' 10.5), to the true nature of human existence as it was revealed 'from the beginning of creation' (10.6). The higher authority given (10.6 f.) to Gen. 1.27; 2.24 over against Deut. 24.1 (v. 4) is not merely an arbitrary decision as to God's will, but is rather an appeal from fallen history to the situation when God's will was done on earth as it is in heaven.[1] Similarly, in the debate about paying tax to Caesar (12.13–17), the contrast between the hard fact of Caesar's dominion illustrated by the coin,[2] and the true nature of the Jewish people and of their destiny, is involved in the answer given. The distinction between the false and the true appeal to the Jewish tradition is also made by the contrast in 11.17. Here the 'den of thieves' with which Jeremiah (7.11) describes the corrupted temple which the Jewish authorities perpetuate stands over against the 'house of prayer for all nations' with which Isa. 56.7 describes the eschatological temple which Jesus brings into existence.

The issue involved in understanding correctly Jesus' teaching is the

---

in correction of the unwarranted claim to the contrary by Albertz, *Die synoptischen Streitgespräche*, 39 (cf. *Die Formeschichte des Evangeliums*, 2nd ed., 224, note 1, not translated in the Eng. ed.). Dibelius' point is to the effect that the passages had in their pre-Marcan form a didactic purpose, and were given their christological orientation only in the Marcan presentation.

[1]Lohmeyer on 10.6–8; Kümmel, 'Jesus und der jüdische Traditionsgedanke', *ZNW*, XXXIII (1934), 124; Stauffer, *TWNT* I, 647 f.; Jeremias, *Jesus als Weltvollender*, 64–69.

[2]So Klostermann; Lohmeyer; Str-B, I, 884.

'kingdom of God' (10.23, 25; 12.34), and those who have not been given the 'mystery of the kingdom of God' 'hear but do not understand' (4.11 f.). At the basis of the struggle between Jesus and the Jewish authorities is their rejection of the kingdom Jesus proclaimed (1.15) and of the 'repentance' for which that proclamation called. Therefore their attitude toward history must consist in a traditionalism which devalues the present and permits only the freedom of an interpreter of the tradition. They must be irrevocably opposed to an eschatological understanding of history which involves basic change as well as continuity, eschatological newness as well as oldness.[1] It is precisely the presence of God's reign which makes possible both the separation from frozen tradition and the deliverance from immanent relativism. God's reign is therefore the basis of Jesus' action in the Marcan debates.

C. TEACHING AND ACTION IN MARK

The close association which has become evident between the debates and the exorcisms is simply one instance of a pervasive trend in Mark to associate the words and action of Jesus. Thus Mark gives a unity to Jesus' ministry which has often been ignored in modern presentations of Jesus.[2] Mark frequently associates the exorcisms and healings on the one hand with Jesus' teaching on the other: 'doing' and 'teaching' (6.30); 'teaching' and 'mighty works' (6.2); 'teaching' and exorcising (1.27); 'preaching' and exorcising by disciples (1.39; 3.14); 'preaching' and exorcising and healing by disciples (6.12 f.); a healing as the content of 'preaching' by the cured person (7.36). The importance of these passages is increased by the fact that a number of them occur in summaries originating with Mark.

In several of the Marcan narratives, words and action have been united because they tend to explain each other. Authoritative action confirms the authority of Jesus' word: Jesus' 'authoritative' teaching in the synagogue (1.21 f.) is clarified by the 'authority' in his word of exorcism (1.23–28); his 'authority' to forgive sin is revealed by the healing action of his word (2.1–12); the execution of the command to the fig tree (11.12–14, 20–24) surrounds the authoritative word at the cleansing of the temple (11.15–19), and this whole unit of authoritative action (cf. esp. 11.23 f.) introduces the final group of debates. It is clear

[1]Cf. Behm in *TWNT*, III, 451.
[2]But cf., e.g., Gerhard Kittel, *TB*, VII (1928), col. 249.

that for Mark the authority of Jesus' teaching resides not in its force of logic or the originality and profundity of its contents, but rather in the power inherent in him as Son of God and bearer of the Spirit, a power which is revealed by the efficacy of his word. When he speaks, God acts: in casting out a demon, in healing a paralytic, in forgiving sin, in addressing his people at worship. This is what cannot, according to Mark, be said of the words of the scribes (1.22). For Jesus' word is action.[1]

Even the larger blocks of Marcan teaching do not provide a haven of refuge for contemplating eternal truths apart from the cosmic struggle taking place in history. Rather the subject matter of these units is that historical struggle itself. The collection of parables has as its prelude the 'parables' of the Beelzebub debate (3.22-30, esp. 23). The interpretation of the main parable of the sower reveals that the 'word' is involved in the struggle with Satan (4.15). Mark allegorizes the parable, but not in the sense of Philo or the medieval allegories: he does not change an eschatological parable of action into moralizing eternal truths; rather he correctly interprets the parables as referring to the historical struggle and its outcome. He simply amplifies the details of that struggle beyond what was envisaged in the parable, thereby revealing his own understanding of history. This understanding is a 'mystery' which is eschatological in nature ('the kingdom of God'), and 'given' by God (4.11) through Jesus (1.15). This same understanding of the historical struggle with Satan and its outcome is the gist of the Marcan apocalypse (ch. 13). This apocalypse is not primarily concerned with speculating about the end (vv. 14-27), but rather with the struggles of the present time (vv. 5-13), the help of the Spirit (v. 11), and the exhortation to watch (vv. 28-37). It sets the frame of reference for understanding the passion narrative and the experience of the Church. The same function is performed by the only extended ethical teaching in Mark: the three discourses on suffering and humility (8.34-37; 9.33-10.31 *passim*; 10.35-45), which follow upon the three predictions of the cross (8.31; 9.31; 10.33 f.).

From the content of the Marcan teaching it is clear that the con-

---

[1]G. Sevenster, *De Christologie van het Nieuwe Testament,* 2. Druk, 1948, 33, cites as instances of Jesus' 'word of might': 1.25, 41; 3.5; 4.39; 5.34, 41; 7.34; 9.25. Then he makes the interesting observation that the saying can be replaced by an action: (1.41); 3.10; 5.28; 8.22. Cf. also 1.31.

fusion of men's minds is a power over man requiring divine action to be overcome (4.11): 'To you is *given* the mystery of the kingdom of God'. The Pharisaic questions are related to the 'hardness' of their hearts (3.5; 10.5). This mental confusion is also identified as Satanic temptation (8.11; 10.2; 12.15). Thus the mental problem which confronts us in the teaching of Jesus is parallel to that which in the exorcisms is due to the presence of an evil spirit or demon.

D. THE DEBATES WITH THE DISCIPLES

Out of the three formal and parallel announcements of the passion (8.31; 9.31; 10.33 f.) there arises a type of debate with the disciples (8.32–9.1; 9.33–50; 10.35–45). Here the opposition of viewpoint is so great as to distinguish these debates from normal discussions between master and disciple, and to bring them into the present context of debates with the Jewish authorities.

The attitude of the disciples with regard to the passion had been anticipated by their failure to understand the two feedings. Here they had already been associated with the Jewish authorities (8.15). They are warned to avoid, in connexion with the feedings, the leaven of the Pharisees and of Herod. The disciples' failure to understand the meaning of the feedings is due in each case to the hardening of their hearts (6.52; 8.17), just as the Jewish authorities harden their hearts (3.5; 10.5). The disciples' lack of understanding is accentuated (6.52; 8.17, 21), and described (8.18) in Old Testament language similar to that used of the crowds (4.12; 7.18).

The attitude of the disciples with regard to the passion is introduced as Satanic (8.33), and at its culmination this attitude is put in the same context of 'temptation' (14.38) as had been the debates with the Jewish authorities. By yielding to Satan's temptation the disciples join the Jewish authorities in the cosmic struggle of Satan against Jesus which began at the temptation in the wilderness, continued in the struggle with demoniacs, advances through the historical context of these debates to right and left, and reaches its climax in the crucifixion and resurrection.

These debates with the disciples have as their main theme the effort of the disciples to dissuade Jesus from the passion, and the false understanding of discipleship which they thereby reveal. We do not have to do simply with two opposing theories of the Messiah, but rather with two understandings of eschatological existence as a whole. For the discussion of the sufferings of the Son of Man easily shifts to a debate about the rôle of the disciples in relation to the kingdom (8.34–37; 9.33–47; 10.35–44), and just as easily shifts back to witnessing to the Son of Man and his future coming in the kingdom of God (8.38–9.1), to the kingdom of God and Gehenna (9.42–50), and to the Son of Man giving his life a ransom for many (10.45).

The unity of Jesus' viewpoint in this section is in terms of the cosmic struggle, so that his teaching to the disciples is parallel to his own action, and both are in eschatological perspective. There his ethical teachings are constantly parallel to christological or eschatological affirmations upon which they are modelled. Similarly the disciples are presented as consistent in their theology and ethics. The attitude which leads to Peter's theological objection to the passion (8.32), leads also to the ethically unworthy discussion among the disciples as to who is greater (9.34), to the unwillingness of the disciples to grant recognition to a new believer (9.38), to the request of James and John for places next to Jesus in his glory (10.35 ff.), and to the anger of the other ten against them (10.41). The disciples are throughout displaying the attitude due to the temptation of Satan (8.33). Thus the submission of Peter to Satan in the question of the messianic theology is carried on in the inability of Peter, James and John to ward off temptation in Gethsemane (14.38), and expresses itself in the flight of all (14.50), followed by the triple denial of Peter (14.66–72). Thus the unity of the disciples' theology, ethics, and action is maintained to the end. Their opposition to Jesus' idea of suffering corresponds to their own unwillingness to suffer, and this in turn blocks their participation in the eschatological history which Jesus awaits in Gethsemane in definitive fashion. The sharpness of the debates of Jesus with the disciples is due to the fact that the issue at stake is Mark's eschatological understanding of history, which he sees advocated and exemplified by Jesus, but opposed in word and deed by the disciples.

This survey of the Marcan material has made it clear that Mark sees the history of Jesus from an eschatological perspective. For Mark the driving force in history is the divine power of the end of time, operative already in the history of Jesus, propelling the whole course of history toward its ultimate destiny. Mark can designate this divine reality in history as the Spirit which cast Jesus into the wilderness to be tempted by Satan, and as the 'authority' (1.22, 27; 2.10; 3.15; 6.7; 11.28 f., 33) or eschatological (9.1; 12.24; 13.26; 14.62) 'power' (5.30; 6.2, 5, 14) with which Jesus carried on this struggle against the demons (1.27; 3.15; 6.7; 9.39), disease (2.10; 5.30; 6.5), and the Jewish authorities (1.22; 2.10; 11.28 f., 33; 12.24). The effect of this divine reality is Jesus' ability to maintain the struggle without attempting to break it off: on the road to Jerusalem (9.30; 10.1, 32 f., 46; 11.1–11), in Gethsemane (14.36, 39, 41 f.), at the trial (14.61 f.; 15.2, 5), and on the cross (15.23, 30–32). This divine reality in history is the basis for both the doctrinal and the ethical correction of the disciples, and is the norm by which their conduct is evaluated. The history which Mark selects to record is presented in its unity as the eschatological action of God, prepared by John the Baptist, inaugurated at the baptism and temptation, carried on through the struggles with various forms of evil, until in his death Jesus has experienced the ultimate of historical involvement and of diabolic antagonism. In the resurrection the force of evil is conclusively broken and the power of God's reign is established in history. It is in this way that Mark understands Jesus' history. The question which still remains is as to how he understands the history in which he himself lives, subsequent to the victory of Christ, yet still among the evils of human history.

V

HISTORY SINCE A.D. 30 IN MARK

A. THE RELEVANCE OF THE QUESTION

A number of years intervene between the history Mark records and the writing of that history by Mark. In order to establish Mark's understanding of history, it is necessary to investigate his understanding of this subsequent period of 'history since A.D. 30'. For if the understanding of history which has been detected in Mark's Gospel were confined to the brief period of Jesus' public ministry, it would be unwarranted to speak in a generalizing way of that understanding as an understanding of 'history'. One would have to say that this was Mark's understanding of Jesus' history, or Mark's understanding of Jesus' biography, or Mark's understanding of Jesus. Only if it becomes clear that the understanding of history evident in the treatment of Jesus is carried over into the interpretation of other history as well, can one speak of it as Mark's understanding of history as such.

It has become clear from the study of Mark's form of presentation that he is not an objective, disinterested historian, but rather an inward participant in the history he narrates. But this does not necessarily imply that he conceives of his own time as a continuation of the kind of history which characterized Jesus' experience. Jesus' experience was for Mark not inconclusive; rather the gospel reached its dramatic climax in Jesus' vindication at the resurrection. Jesus triumphs in the struggle; is not the struggle then at an end? Certainly Jesus' struggle and his resurrection have for Mark saving significance. But this significance could be focused by Mark in either of two directions. The believer could be saved out of such a historical struggle as characterized Jesus' career; or he could be saved in that struggle, i.e., freed by Jesus' victory to continue fruitfully in the struggle on to the end, with a power and steadfast hope previously lacking to the disciples.

It is this second alternative which finds expression in such a concise statement as 10.30: 'Now in this time a hundredfold houses and brothers and sisters and mothers and children and lands, with persecutions; and in the age to come eternal life.' Mark speaks of the age to come (and the apocalyptic drama) as still future, in spite of Jesus' resurrection and the eschatological existence of the believer. This cannot be ignored as an irrelevant vestige of Jewish language. By ignoring this fact one could identify the present eschatological existence with the new aeon, and therefore describe this existence as non-historical, just as the new aeon of apocalypticism is envisaged as non-historical.[1] Mark too conceives of the new aeon in non-historical terms. But when he carefully distinguishes the existence of the Church from that non-historical aeon and defines the Church as within the present evil aeon, he is defining its existence as historical.

The non-historicity of the apocalyptic view of the new aeon

[1]This is the basic error, at least if applied to Mark, of Bultmann's tendency, 'History and Eschatology in the New Testament', 5 ff., to identify the apocalyptic view of the end of history (in distinction to the OT prophetic view of a goal of history) with the Christian understanding of the present. The apocalyptic view is stated, 7: 'History comes to an end with the ending of the old aeon. The state of welfare belongs to the new aeon, in which, according to IV Ezra 7.31, vanity vanishes, and according to Slav. Enoch 65.7, 8, times and years will be annihilated and months and days and hours will be no more.' Even if Mark envisages such a state for the 'aeon to come', he does not interpret the present in these terms. Cf. Wilhelm Michaelis' justified emphasis upon the fact that the NT does not speak of the coming aeon as having come, and his criticism of such terms as *Aeonenwende* to designate the meaning of the resurrection: 'Zur Frage der Aeonenwende', *TB*, XVIII (1939), col. 113–18. This is not to be confused with the question whether there is for Mark eschatological occurrence in the present. For Mark there certainly is; but it is eschatological occurrence in history, the 'present aeon'. Bultmann is also incorrect in citing (8) Mark 9.43, 45 on the coming 'life' as descriptions of the present, when Mark 10.29 f. makes it clear that this non-historical 'life' (Bultmann, 9, cites Mark 12.25) is not a description of the present, but of the future. Although it is true that for Mark national history has ceased to be the framework for salvation, the believer is still within history. Mark does not deny that history has meaning (Bultmann, 16: 'Henceforth history must no longer be understood as saving history, but as profane history.'); rather he repudiates a completely negative understanding of history, and achieves an understanding of history as composed of the struggle between Spirit and Satan. According to Mark's understanding of history it would not be correct to say that with the apocalyptic arrival of the new aeon history had come to an end, i.e., been repudiated; it would be more accurate to say that history would then reach its goal, the outcome of the struggle.

consisted largely in the absence of pain, suffering and evil. Suffering is however a central part of Mark's understanding of his existence. By defining the Church's existence as a combination of eschatological blessing and persecution, Mark is distinguishing it on the one hand from the non-eschatological history preceding Jesus, and on the other hand from the non-historicity of the new aeon. Mark's understanding of the Church is rooted in a new understanding of history as the interplay of blessedness and suffering. This new understanding of history is rooted in the event in history through which a new situation in history is inaugurated. In the present chapter this thesis is to be confirmed from the various allusions in Mark to history after A.D. 30.

B. THE TEMPORAL LIMITS OF THE MARCAN HISTORY

The Gospel of Mark covers a very brief span of time. In the debate as to the length of the public ministry of Jesus, the Marcan presentation has usually been held to favour a one-year ministry. This fact has been used to question the appropriateness of designating Mark as a biography of Jesus. It raises all the more the question as to whether we have to do in Mark with a 'history'. It is at least valid to ask how far the portrayal of so brief a period can be generalized into an understanding of history as a whole.

The analysis of the Marcan introduction made it clear that the late beginning of Mark (in comparison, e.g., with the beginnings of Matt. and Luke) was intentional, and was not due to the external cause of the absence of information as to Jesus' and John's previous experience. Rather the abrupt beginning with John's preparatory baptism and the baptism of Jesus involved a relative evaluation of history prior to and subsequent to John. Mark began where he began because a new kind of history on a higher level began at that point. One cannot do justice to Mark's understanding of history by ignoring this fact. One cannot assume that what he says of Jesus' ministry was also true for him with regard to antecedent history.

The ending of Mark is unfortunately too obscure to permit of a similar analysis as to the significance of the point at which Mark drew his narrative to a close. The allusion in 16.7 to 'going before you into Galilee' (cf. 14.28) is subject to interpretations which would support each side of the debate on 'history after A.D. 30'. Lohmeyer[1] sees in the

[1] *Galiläa und Jerusalem*, 10–14.

reference an allusion to the *parousia,* so that no meaningful history would be mentioned between the resurrection and the *parousia.* On the other hand C. F. Evans[1] revives a suggestion by Hoskyns to the effect that a prediction of the gentile mission is intended, so that Mark would, like Luke, conceive of a post-resurrection history of Jesus acting through the Church. The traditional view[2] is to the effect that Mark understood the saying as referring to resurrection appearances. The statement in 16.7 is itself unclear, and the various interpretations have resorted to the general Marcan presentation for the defence of their positions. Conjectures as to the contents of a 'lost ending' of Mark cannot be made sufficiently likely to provide a basis for discussion.[3] On the other hand the ending of Mark at 16.8 is still too unproven to serve as a basis for theological deductions, which would at best be arguments from silence. Ultimately such a view would also rest upon evidence drawn from the body of Mark's Gospel rather than from the obscure ending. The most that can be said is that Mark, as we have it, covers only a brief period of time. Thus the narrow scope of the period presented by Mark does pose a problem which must be met before his understanding of history as a whole can be discussed.

In view of the distinction reflected in the Marcan introduction between history prior to John and history subsequent to John, an examination of Marcan allusions to prior history is in place. This examination will make it clear that the Marcan distinction is not the sharp rejection of Jewish history which is found, e.g., in Marcion or the Epistle of Barnabas. In the introduction Mark began deliberately with a Jewish prophet, whose appearance was itself the fulfilment of the prophecy of Isaiah. For to maintain, as Mark does maintain (specifically: 1.2; 7.6; 9.12 f.; 11.17; 12.10, 36; 14.49), that he is recording the fulfilment of Jewish prophecy, has in it a positive as well as a negative evaluation of Jewish history. That history is only

---

[1] "I will Go Before You into Galilee," ' *JTS,* n.s. V (1954), 3 ff.

[2] Cf., e.g., J. Weiss, *The History of Primitive Christianity,* I, 14 ff.

[3] As early as B. Weiss, *Das Marcusevangelium und seine synoptischen Parallelen,* 1872, 54, the classification of resurrection appearances as beyond the Marcan concept of a Gospel raised the question as to whether Mark wrote a book of Acts later used by Luke in the first half of his Acts. Such a view was advocated by Friedrich Blass, *Philology of the Gospels,* 1898, 141 ff.; F. C. Burkitt, *Christian Beginnings,* 1924, 83; W. K. Lowther Clarke, 'The Ending of St. Mark', *Theology,* XXIX (1934), 106 f.

preliminary, in that its truth is that of prophecy. Yet as such it is preparatory, and by the fulfilment of the prophecy it receives its vindication.
However it could be argued that, as in the case, e.g., of the *Epistle of
Barnabas*, the prophetic value of the Old Testament could be combined
with a rejection of Jewish history, on the basis that Judaism misunder-
stood or rejected the prophecy given to it (cf., e.g., Mark 7.6 f.; 12.2–5).
The prophecy would not be envisaged as part of Jewish history, but as
judgement upon Jewish history. Nevertheless it is in the person of the
rejected prophet that the situation prior to Jesus is most similar to
Jesus' history, and to the history of the Church. Perhaps the nearest
that Mark comes to a universal in his interpretation of history is that
persecution is an indispensable part of the godly life. The Jewish
prophets have this in common with Jesus[1] (12.2–8); John the Baptist
has it in common with Jesus (9.11–13);[2] the Christian has it in common
with Jesus (10.38 f.). Therefore there is an important link connecting the
two periods set apart by Mark: the persecuted witness (cf. I Thess. 2.14–16).

Furthermore Mark's use of the Old Testament is not confined to
prophecy. Old Testament laws are recognized as valid (7.10; 10.7 f.,
19; 12.29–33). When the Pharisees, Jews, elders, and traditions are
rejected, it is by appeal to Moses (7.1 ff.); when Moses is rejected, it is
by appeal to the creation narrative in the first book of Moses (10.2 ff.).
Nor is Jewish history seen merely from the point of view of divine
prophecy and legislation. It contains for Mark historical incidents
which are exemplary, as, e.g., the incident taken from the life of the
greatest Israelite king (2.25 f.). God is 'the God of Abraham and the
God of Isaac and the God of Jacob' (12.26); Jesus is the 'son of David'
(12.47); the coming kingdom is 'David's' (11.10); John is 'Elijah'
(9.13). It is evident that the distinction which Mark makes between
Jewish history and the time of Jesus is not such as to destroy all
positive meaning of past history.

Once the distinction between Jesus' history and antecedent history
has been clarified so as to prevent a Marcionite interpretation of that
distinction, the investigation can turn to a positive definition of the
difference between the two periods. When one examines Mark's under-

---

[1] Cf. Leonhard Goppelt, *Typos*, 1939, 92.

[2] Cf. Lightfoot, *History and Interpretation in the Gospels*, 92 f.; 'In 9.11–13 we
may perhaps see the church striving to construct some kind of a philosophy
of history, in the light of its convictions about the person and office of its
Master, of his work and its results.'

standing of history prior to John the Baptist, it is apparent that Mark does not see there the cosmic struggle between the Spirit and Satan which he sees in Jesus' history. The baptism of Jesus with the Spirit and his temptation by Satan in the wilderness present for Mark a *novum* in history. History after this time is essentially different, on a more meaningful and intense plane than before; Mark's understanding of history cannot be reduced to a rational theory of either a moralistic or Hegelian variety. He does not mean simply that in Jesus' history the principle of all history is revealed, so that once this meaning has been learned it can be identified anywhere in any period. The Spirit comes into history upon Jesus. Similarly Jesus in preaching the nearness of the kingdom is not speaking simply of an abstract truth, namely the inescapability of God, but is referring to an event in the near future. Just as the Jewish eschatological hope envisaged a form of human existence different from historical existence as we know it (cf. the cessation of marriage 12.25), the messianic history of Jesus is conceived of by Mark as a different form of human existence from that of preceding history.

It will be the objective of the following section to demonstrate that the Marcan eschatology is such as to imply a continuation within the Church of the same kind of history as characterized Jesus' history, i.e., a struggle between the Spirit and Satan, until the final outcome of that struggle is reached and the goal of history attained. However, assuming such an outcome of the following investigation, a further question remains with regard to the Marcan distinction of history B.C. and A.D. To what extent can an understanding of history which applies only to the Christian era, and perhaps only to those parts of history in the Christian era where the Church is present, be envisaged as an understanding of history as such, and not merely an understanding of Christian history, or of Church history? Apparently Mark would not use the 'understanding of history' evident in his Gospel for treating the history of earlier times or other cultures. In this sense his understanding of history is not intended as a tool for the scholarly historian. But it is at this point that one must recall that although Mark himself can be called a 'historian' in the sense that he is a writer of historical occurrences and their meaning, he is himself not a scholarly historian, in terms of research and objectivity. His book is not a 'document' or a 'source', but rather a 'witness', a 'Gospel'. It is not intended as enlightenment for the scholar as scholar, but rather as guidance for man as man. The understanding of history which Mark provides is the understanding of history which applies to each reader of his Gospel. As a key to the historical experience of the reader, Mark's understanding of history is universal. That is to say: As an interpretation of history written and read in the Christian era and by those within the Church or who encounter the Church, it is of validity for every reader who is attempting to understand the history in which he finds himself. This existential form of universality which characterizes Mark's understanding of history is rooted in the fact that Mark envisages the cosmic struggle as extending to all peoples and continuing to the culmination of history. Mark's understanding of history shares in the universality of the cosmic struggle itself.

C. THE MARCAN APOCALYPSE

Although we must for the purposes of discussion assume that Mark's Gospel terminated with the resurrection, we are not left completely without references to the future. As a matter of fact, the book characterizes itself as eschatologically orientated by the quantity of references to the future event bringing history to its consummation. This event is envisaged by Mark as a future event in time and space (cf. 13.32; 'day and hour'; 13.33: 'the time'). It is now generally recognized that the kingdom which Jesus preached was envisaged primarily as future, with its present activity as the exception to or as the anticipation of the future completeness. The distinctiveness of the future coming is particularly accentuated in 9.1 by the description of that coming as 'in power'. Through the association with the immediately preceding verse (8.38), this coming of the kingdom is identified with a coming of the Son of Man, which is also distinguished from Jesus' present coming by the characterization: 'in the glory of his father with the holy angels'. Similarly the distinctiveness of the future coming of the Son of Man is described (13.26): 'in clouds with much power and glory'. Only with this event does the radical transformation take place (13.27). Therefore descriptions which are of a clearly non-historical nature[1] must be placed after that event. It is the

[1] 12.25: 'When they rise from the dead, they neither marry nor are given in marriage, but are like angels in heaven'; 13.31; 'heaven and earth will pass away'; 9.43–47: 'life' (43, 45) or 'the kingdom of God' (47) as the alternative to 'gehenna'; 10.30: 'eternal life' as characteristic of 'the coming age' in distinction from now in 'this time'.

central importance of this final future event as a fixed point on the horizon which gives to the outlook of Mark a horizontality, a temporality, which distinguishes Mark from the mystery religions, which tend to direct attention inward or upward, out of time into eternity. The fact of the future event produces the attitude of alertness with regard to the events of time and space which finds expression in the repeated admonitions to 'watch' (13.34, 35, 37), 'take heed' (13.5, 9, 23, 33), 'stay awake' (13.33). The future event is but the completion of the eschatological history of Jesus which Mark has recorded, as is evident from the continuity of the concepts of the kingdom and of the Son of Man from Jesus' history to the *parousia*. This tends to give the intervening period its orientation (cf., e.g., 2.20), and to suggest the interpretation of that period in terms of the struggle with which it begins and the final victory with which it terminates. It is this suggestion which finds its confirmation in the Marcan apocalypse.

The modern history of the interpretation of the Marcan apocalypse[1] has revolved around two inescapable facts: (1) The Marcan apocalypse at times clings to the language of prophecy, providing a more visible identification in the history of Jewish apocalyptic language than in the course of historical events. (2) The Marcan apocalypse at times fits the events of first century history and of the book of Acts so completely that it seems to be history written in the form of a *vaticinium ex eventu*. Unfortunately the significance of this tension for the understanding of Mark has been largely lost in the debate as to whether the Marcan apocalypse is a real prophecy (whence the stereotyped language and its historical vagueness), or is actually a *vaticinium ex eventu* (whence its historical clarity), or is perhaps a combination of the two (whence the tension). Irrespective of the way in which the origin of the Marcan apocalypse be explained, the tension itself exists, and must be interpreted as such in an interpretation of Mark.

1. On the one hand we have to do with history written in the form of *prophecy*. The Church is specifically exhorted (13.23) to find the meaning of its historical experience in terms of the fact: 'I have told you all things beforehand.' It is therefore no accident that the history of the Church is present in the form of a prophecy. History which occurs according to prophecy is history with God-given meaning. To call upon the Church to interpret its history as prophesied is to call upon

[1]This history is thoroughly presented by G. R. Beasley-Murray, *Jesus and the Future*, 1954.

the Church to interpret its history theologically. Furthermore it is of considerable relevance for Mark that the prophecy comes from Jesus: the history of the Church proceeds from, is given by, Jesus. This is the significance of the fact that motifs in the apocalypse are often echoes of important passages from the narrative concerning Jesus.[1] It is clear that the experiences of the Church are presented in the Marcan apocalypse as prophesied by and modelled after the history of Jesus.

2. The other aspect of the tension in the Marcan apocalypse is the fact that the prophecy has to do with events of *history*. The fact that Mark sees his life lifted up into a theological dimension by the redemptive action of the heavenly Lord does not eliminate the fact that this theologically understood life is seen as historical experience. When Matthew and Luke accentuate the historicity of the narrative more than does Mark,[2] they are only continuing a trend already present in Mark. For Mark provides both temporal sequence (13.7, 8, 10, 14, 21, 24, 26, 27) and language descriptive of present history (13.9 ff.).[3] The experience of the Church depicted in the apocalypse involves such matters of

[1]Parallels have been drawn to the Marcan parables (3.20–4.34) by Lightfoot, *The Gospel Message of St. Mark*, 40; Farrer, *A Study in St. Mark*, 164–6; to the three predictions of the passion and the subsequent definitions of discipleship (chs. 8–10) by Busch, *Zum Verständnis der synoptischen Eschatologie*, 39 ff.; and to the passion narrative esp. by Lohmeyer, 'Die Reinigung des Tempels', *TB*, XX (1941), 257–64, summarized by Lightfoot, *The Gospel Message of St. Mark*, 48–59. For further parallels see below.

[2]Matthew, e.g., by adding temporal terms so as to heighten the sense of sequence (24.9, 10, 14, 29), Luke by using language which points to historical facts such as the fall of Jerusalem (21.20–24).

[3]Günther Harder, 'Das eschatologische Geschichtsbild der sogenannten kleinen Apokalypse Markus 13', *Theologia Viatorum* IV (1952), 71–107, distinguished sharply between Mark's and Luke's 'view of history'. Luke gives an 'interpretation [of Mark 13.14–20] from contemporary history' (91), and in general 'engages in an eschatological interpretation of history', i.e., his presentation is 'determined by contemporary events and their prophetic interpretation in the Church' (101). Mark sees the destruction of the temple 'precisely not as a political event, but as an occurrence which goes beyond the dimensions of the historical and therefore as eschatological' (103), a drama set off by the death and resurrection of Jesus (102). But Harder's sharp distinction breaks down on his concession (98) that Mark's 'subject-matter' is 'the historical event of the expansion of the Christian Church and her conflict with synagogue and State government'. Nor is it accurate from Mark's point of view to speak of his presentation as 'exceeding the dimensions of the historical', since Mark's understanding of history is throughout

public and official nature as courtroom proceedings (13.9, 11), international wars (13.7 f.), and messianic pretenders (13.5 f., 21 f.).[1] The Church is seen as involved in experiences which are historical in nature, although these historical experiences are prophesied by Jesus, interpreted in the light of his experience, and seen as a commentary upon the exhortation to take up one's cross and follow him. The Christian is called upon to understand his history, not just his mystic or cultic experience, in the same way as he understands the history of Jesus. The statement (13.11) that the Holy Spirit will guide Christians in their defence before hostile courts is merely a confirmation of the fact which is already evident, that the struggle between the Spirit and Satan continues in the history of the Church.

D. THE CHURCH OF JEWS AND GENTILES

The fact that the Marcan Apocalypse presents events of Church history in the form of a prophecy from Jesus provides the key for interpreting the aspects of Jesus' history which also have a *Sitz im Leben* in Church history. Previous scholarship has found primarily two ways of explaining such parallels. The cult relived in a mystic way experiences of Jesus' history; or the apologetic pragmatism involved in the Church's struggle for existence (viewed from a completely immanent point of view) led to basing various customs of the Church in incidents of Jesus' life. Neither of these solutions takes account of Mark's eschatological understanding of history, which sees Jesus and the Church engaged in the same cosmic struggle against the same demonic force of evil.

---

eschatological, as Harder himself emphasizes (99). To be sure, if Harder means here by the 'historical' a modern definition such as the 'non-miraculous', then Mark exceeds the 'historical'—but then so also does the whole NT. The sharpness of Harder's antithesis between Mark and Luke is also blunted by the concession that Mark 13.10 'stands near to the Lucan conception' (104 f., and that Luke 21. 34–36 is 'a fragment of the older [Mark] eschatological view of history' (97). Cf. Conzelmann, *Die Mitte der Zeit*, 108. But even as Harder's antithesis stands, it does not correspond to the Bultmannian antithesis bewteen Paul and Luke. For Harder maintains that both Mark and Luke have eschatological views of history and he presents Luke's as largely dependent on Rom. 11.25 (101). Harder's presentation contains little which could not be explained by the fact (presupposed 104) that Mark wrote before, and Luke after, the destruction of Jerusalem.

[1] Cf. further Busch, *Zum Verständnis der synoptischen Eschatologie*, 62.

It would denote a secularizing modernization in one's understanding of the early Church, to assume that its appeal to Jesus in explaining its action was a *post facto* procedure brought on only by the opposition the Church encountered. Rather the action of the Church was motivated by its faith, and opposition was inherently awaited from such action. When then the Church appeals to Jesus in its debates, it is merely bringing into the open the understanding of its action latent in its faith.

If on the other hand the eucharist and other 'cult legends' were the only part of the life of the Church which Mark traced back to scenes in the life of Jesus, one could argue that the history of the Church (in distinction from its cultic mysteries) was not necessarily understood in terms of Jesus' history. But the missionary activity of the Church is traced back to the lifetime and initiative of Jesus (3.13 ff.; 6.7 ff., 30). This missionary activity of the disciples in Mark, consisting of voyages, hardships, healings, exorcisms, and witnessing (the same ingredients as compose the history of Jesus), must be described as historical experiences. This can be particularly illustrated by the fact that one historical event of great world-historical importance is likewise rooted by Mark in the history of Jesus: the success of the gentile mission.

The shift of Christianity from Palestine and a Jewish membership to the whole Mediterranean world and an inter-racial membership is a well established fact in the history of the period between Jesus' life and the time when Mark wrote his Gospel. The impact of this historical fact[1] upon Mark is not only obvious from indications suggesting that he himself lived outside Palestine,[2] but also from the importance of gentiles and non-Jewish territory in his Gospel (esp. chs. 6–8). The necessity, e.g., of explaining (7.3 f.), a Jewish custom to the reader and the way in which this explanation is stated ('For the Pharisees and all the Jews . . .') indicate that Mark does not understand himself and his reader as falling within Judaism, either theologically or culturally. The discussion with the Syrophoenician woman (7.24–30) can only be understood in terms of a historical process envisaged on the pattern 'first the Jews and then the gentiles', a pattern whose

[1]G. H. Boobyer, 'Galilee and Galileans in St. Mark's Gospel', *BJRL*, XXV (1952–3), 340, lists as 'possible allusions' to the gentile mission: 1.17; 4.23; 10.45; 11.17; 14.24; and as 'definite' allusions: 12.9; 13.10, 27; 14.9.
[2]Cf. B. W. Bacon, *Is Mark a Roman Gospel?* 1919.

existence in the early Church is thoroughly documented in Paul and
Luke-Acts.

The rejection of Jewish custom (7.1 ff.) can only be understood
correctly when one realizes that Mark rejects gentile custom in equally
categorical terms (10.42). It is clear that we do not have to do in
Mark with some racial or national preference, but rather with some
third viewpoint from which all past custom can be rejected. The evidence can best be explained in terms of the Christian's eschatological
awareness of being distinct from the historical custom of the present
evil aeon, whereby it becomes irrelevant whether that custom be
Jewish or gentile. The association of the gentiles with the Jews in the
guilt for executing Jesus[1] is to be understood in terms of the classification of the whole generation to which Jesus came as the present evil
aeon.[2] Similarly Paul associates both Jew and gentile in guilt under the
law (Rom. 1–3), or under the στοιχεῖα (Col. 3.8, 20; Gal. 4.3), so that
all the executioners of Jesus can be brought together as under the
sway of 'the rulers of this age' (I Cor. 2.8). The same association
of Jews and gentiles is also envisaged by Mark in the persecution of
Christians (13.9), a further indication of the correspondence which
exists between his theological understanding of Jesus' history and of
the Church's history. Both Jesus and the Church bear the Spirit within
the present evil aeon, and consequently suffer at its hands.

It is clear that the presence of gentiles in the Church is understood
theologically by Mark. They are really no longer 'gentiles', but
Christians. Yet within this theological appraisal is included the
historical fact that the gentiles have since the history of Jesus entered
into the Church in such proportions as to put them alongside the Jews
in the saving significance and prophetic meaning of the history of
Jesus. This would seem to be the suggestion of the two feedings, in so
far as the numbers 12 and 7 are given special prominence (8.19 f.) and
may be associated with the communion of the Jews and gentiles (cf.
e.g., Acts 6.1 ff.).[3] There are also indications that Mark sees in the

---

[1]Mark is noticeably more reticent in exonerating Pilate than are Matt.
(27.19, 22, 24 f.) and Luke (23.4, 20, 22, 25).
[2]Cf. 8.12, 38; 9.19; 13.30 and Büchsel, *TWNT*, I, 661.
[3]Cf. G. H. Boobyer, 'The Miracles of the Loaves and the Gentiles in St.
Mark's Gospel', *SJT*, VI (1953), 80 ff. Cf. also Lightfoot, *History and Interpretation in the Gospels,* 182–205.

death of Jesus a particular significance for the admission of the gentiles.[1]

The various traces within Mark of a pattern of history including as an important aspect the entrance of the gentiles into the Church are brought together into a unified presentation by the parable of the wicked tenants (12.1–11). The introduction of the vineyard theme in the language of Isa. 5.2 makes it clear that the parable's vineyard is, from the first verse on, understood as the people of God. In the Marcan parable the Jewish people—either as a whole or in the person of their leaders—have repeatedly rejected God's servants, until by rejecting his Son they are themselves rejected.[2] Thus they lose the 'inheritance' they sought (v. 7), and it is turned over to 'others' (v. 9). These 'others' are obviously the Christians, and while it would be too much to say that a Church composed only of gentiles is intended,[3] to say the least this understanding of the Church presupposes the rejection of the Jews and thus by implication the inclusion of the gentiles. Furthermore the course of the parable has for Mark the significance of a sketch of history, so that it confirms the pattern of the course of history which has already been sensed in Mark and which is every-where presupposed in his understanding of the nature of history: There is the time of the prophets, followed by the time of Jesus, which is followed by the time of the Church. The former two times have in common for Mark a prophetic significance, but are separated by the point at which the fulfilment begins; the latter two times have in common for him the struggle of the Spirit *versus* Satan, but are separated by the point at which the decisive victory takes place.

The result of this investigation into Marcan history after A.D. 30 is

---

[1] This interpretation of Jesus' passion is presented by Lightfoot, *The Gospel Message of St. Mark*, 60–69, and by C. F. Evans, ' "I will Go Before You into Galilee",' *JTS*, n.s., V (1954), 15. Further bibliography is listed by G. H. Boobyer, 'The Miracles of the Loaves and the Gentiles in St. Mark's Gospel', *SJT*, VI (1953), 83, n. 1. Cf. esp. M. Kiddle, 'The Death of Jesus and the Admission of the Gentiles in St. Mark', *JTS*, XXXV (1934), 45 ff.

[2] Mark 4.10–25 may also be the reflection of Mark's awareness of the rejection of the Jews. The passage is in tone parallel to Rom. 9–11, and, in view of the Marcan parable of the vineyard, may reasonably be associated with the theological problem posed by the general failure of the Jewish mission. So Lightfoot, *History and Interpretation in the Gospels*, 76.

[3] With Jülicher, *Die Gleichnisreden Jesus*, II, 403, f.; Goppelt, *Typos*, 92 f.; Kümmel, 'Das Gleichnis von den bösen Wiengartnern', *Aux sources de la tradition chrétienne*, 1950, 128.

that history since the resurrection is conceived of as a continuation of the same cosmic struggle which Jesus began. While this conclusion cannot be used as a proof of such conjectures as a Marcan Church history following 16.8, yet the results attained in the present study should be sufficient to stop exaggerated statements as to the impropriety of Luke's writing the book of Acts, as well as to put in question the antithesis between history and Christianity upon which such criticisms are based.

VI

HISTORICAL ATTITUDE AND
COMMUNAL HISTORY

In the study of 'history since A.D. 30' it has become evident that Mark
understood the history of his own time and experience in the same
way as he understood the history of Jesus. In the present chapter this
conclusion should receive its confirmation and application. For here
the question is to be raised as to the historicity of Mark's own religious
outlook, and as to the nearest historical milieu in which he finds himself. The first question is directed to his definition of 'piety', indicating
the direction of what could perhaps be called a Marcan 'psychology of
religion'. The second question is directed to Mark's definition of
'Church', indicating the direction of what could perhaps be called a
Marcan 'sociology of religion'. This study of his 'stance' toward his
own history and of his 'construction' of that history should provide
the 'subjective' and objective' statements of his own relation to
history.

The method for investigating Mark's own religious attitude is based
upon the following considerations. The Jesus of the story Mark tells
is the heavenly Lord he worships. In the course of the story various
personages assume differing attitudes towards Jesus. As Mark evaluates
these attitudes, he reveals his own attitude. By establishing the attitude
which is for Mark normative, one can establish Mark's own norm of
piety.

A. THE NUMINOUS IN MARK

Expressions of the numinous[1] feeling are undoubtedly frequent in
Mark. These numinous expressions have been identified as the central
Marcan concept of piety by those who have attempted to prove the

[1]For the definition of this term and the philosophy of religion which it
represents, cf. the classic formulation by Rudolf Otto, *The Idea of the Holy*,
2nd ed., 1950. He cites (158) Mark 10.32 as the formulation of this feeling
toward Jesus.

appropriateness of the conclusion at 16.8, a verse containing four numinous expressions.[1] The reaction of scholarship against the historicizing interpretation of the nineteenth century with its low Marcan christology led to an accentuation of the high christology of Mark, which would well correspond with a numinous definition of piety.[2] However the present analysis has served to show that the loftiness of Jesus, although unquestioned by Mark, is not central in his presentation, which is rather concerned with Jesus' struggle, action and suffering. The Marcan Jesus is not *of* history, but on the other hand he is not aloof from history; rather he comes, gives himself into the historical situation, and performs a history-creating function. Therefore the numinous definition of piety is not necessitated by the Marcan view of Jesus.

In 10.32 the disciples follow Jesus to Jerusalem in awe and terror. The basic difficulty in identifying this verse as the centre of Mark's ideal of piety is that this scene falls within the section of debates between Jesus and the disciples about suffering. The attitude of the disciples in 10.32 is parallel to Peter's rebuke to Jesus (8.32), the disciples' discussion as to who is greatest (9.34), their amazement at the difficulty of salvation (10.24, 26,) the request of James and John for places of prestige (10.35, 37), and the indignation of the other ten (10.41). The interest in glory and greatness reflected in this attitude is rejected by Jesus, just as the cowardly fear here so closely associated with this attitude is opposed to the conduct of Jesus.

The nearest parallels to 10.32 in its combination of cowardly fear and numinous awe on the part of the disciples are the two scenes on the sea (4.40 f.; 6.49–52). Both stories begin with cowardly fear and conclude with numinous awe. The intimate association of the two attitudes is evident from the fact that the verb φοβεῖσθαι refers in 4.41 to awe (as in 5.15; 16.8; perhaps 6.20; 9.32), while in 6.50 ('do not fear') it refers to cowardice (as in 5.33, 36; 11.18, 32; 12.12; perhaps 6.20; 9.32). Furthermore both attitudes are attributed to unclarity as to Jesus; fear is due to lack of faith (4.40), confusing Jesus with a ghost

[1] Cf. especially Lindton, 'Der vermisste Markusschluss', *TB*, VIII (1929), col. 229–43.

[2] The interpretation of Ebeling, *Das Messiasgeheimnis und die Botschaft des Marcus-Evangelisten*, brings this implication of the work of Wrede to the forefront. Otto, *The Idea of the Holy*, 159, has rightly seen in the numinous feeling toward Jesus the beginning of the high christology of later centuries.

(6.49), and not knowing that 'it is I' (6.50); awe expresses itself with the question 'Who is he?' (4.41), and is explained (6.52) as follows: 'for they did not understand about the loaves, but their heart was hardened'. (Could Mark add such a commentary to his ideal of piety?) Fear and awe are not here distinguished as one would distinguish non-Christian and Christian attitudes to Jesus, but both are brought together and stand over against the Christian confession of Jesus as Son of God (15.39).

It is true that the first Marcan expression of amazement toward Jesus (1.22, 27) is presented uncritically as a testimony to Jesus. But when Mark comes to a thematic discussion of admiring designations of Jesus (6.14–16; 8.28), it is clear that they do not have his approval. Even the title Messiah must be corrected from its pompous Jewish to its humble Christian meaning (8.29–33). Therefore the synagogue scene (1.23–27) received in Mark a limitation which it may not have had in its oral circulation, and must find its commentary in its nearest Marcan parallel, the synagogue scene of 6.1–6. The amazement of 1.27 is repeated in 6.2; but this amazement is then expounded as offence (v. 3), dishonour (v. 4), an obstacle to the divine action (v. 5), lack of faith (v. 6). Jesus amazes those who know him according to the flesh (v. 3a); but Mark knows him according to the Spirit.

One could expect Mark to attribute his ideal of piety to Jesus, and to withhold it from Jesus' enemies. His usage with regard to fear and awe is just the reverse. In only two instances is such an attitude attributed to Jesus: in his home town when his power fails and he is amazed at their lack of faith (6.5 f.), and in Gethsemane where he is 'amazed and disturbed' (14.33). These are precisely the two passages in Mark where Jesus falls out of his normal rôle as bearer of the Spirit, and stands—like the disciples (cf., e.g., 9.18; 14.38, 50)—over against God, and separated from his eschatological *dynamis* (6.5; 14.36). It is obvious that it was not this attitude of awe which brought forth the history of Jesus which Mark records.

On the other hand both cowardly fear and numinous awe characterize the authorities opposed to Jesus: They 'fear' the crowd (11.32; 12.12), and even 'fear' Jesus (11.18). They do not 'dare' question Jesus further (12.34; contrast 15.43). This 'fear' shifts imperceptibly into 'amazement' with numinous overtones at Jesus' answer to their question as to tax for Caesar (12.17). But such awe does not prevent these authorities from putting Jesus to death, any more than Herod's numinous 'fear' of John (6.20) prevented him from executing John, or Pilate's 'amazement' at Jesus (15.5, 44) prevented the execution. Mark doubtless appreciated the awe in which Jesus was held by his enemies, just as he appreciated the confessions of the demons. But just as the demons were none the less silenced and cast out, the enemies of Jesus remain none the less his enemies. It is therefore inconceivable that an attitude which is applied to Jesus only inconsistently, but which characterizes those who put him to death, could be regarded by Mark as the ideal of piety.

Mark's rejection of awe as a religious ideal may be due to the effect it has of suspending the action of Jesus, and thus of blocking the eschatological history Mark advocates and records. Overawed in the presence of the numen, man shrinks back (5.33). This fear must be overcome before action is possible (5.36). However a numen is not only awesome, but also fascinating,[1] and Mark's Jesus creates not only awe and fear, but also excitement, attention, crowds. If Mark is interested in the historicity of Jesus, it could be this quality of fascination, bringing Jesus to the attention of the authorities and thus into world history, which was of interest to him.

Jesus' great popularity finds expression primarily in the chorus-like reactions on the part of the crowd. This motif has been identified[2] as a stylistic convention of the Hellenistic world for accentuating the completeness of the cure or the greatness of the healer. When one inquires as to Mark's appraisal of this aspect of the material before him, one first observes that in most cases he makes no comment upon the motif, leaving it with its implicit positive significance: 1.22, 27; 2.12; 5.20, 42; 7.37; 11.18; 12.37; etc. However when one investigates Mark's designations of those who give expression to this attitude of fascination, it becomes increasingly difficult to find in them his ideal of piety.

The groups expressing such mass acclaim are not clearly defined, but are variously designated as those in the 'synagogue' (1.21, 23, 29; 6.2), or 'all' (1.27; 2.12; 5.20), or the 'crowd' (11.18; 12.37), or simply

---

[1]Cf. Otto, *The Idea of the Holy*, 31.

[2]Cf. Bultmann, *Die Geschichte der synoptischen Tradition*, 241. Cf. also Lindton, 'Der vermisste Markusschluss', *TB*, VIII (1929), col. 231. The Marcan list given by Bultmann and Lindton could be supplemented by the following passages: 5.15, 20, 33; 6.2; 11.18; 12.37.

'they' (7.37; 5.42).¹ These and other designations for the chorus do not
indicate that Mark looked with favour on this group. The 'synagogue'
is Jesus' habitual place for teaching (1.39; 3.1). Yet it is also the scene
of persecutions to Christians (13.9), and the site of the scribes' pride
(12.39). The 'crowd' of 4.1 is defined (v. 11) as 'those outside' in distinction from the 'twelve', and the 'crowd' is taught in riddles so that
they will not understand and repent (v. 12; cf. also 7.14, 18). The
'crowd' presses Jesus (3.9; 5.24, 31), prevents him from eating (3.20),
obstructs his contact with those he wishes to help (2.4; 5.31). The
'crowd' is hardly for Mark the chosen people, for when it is defined
geographically in terms of Jewish-inhabited areas of Galilee (3.7 f.), it
is the group from which Jesus retires to choose the twelve.² 'Israel'
occurs in Mark only incidentally, in quoting the Shema (12.29), and in
the taunt 'Christ King of Israel', in which scene the taunting Jewish
authorities are hardly for Mark the holy people of God. Jerusalem is
the source of 'crowds' (3.7 f.), but this city is itself appraised as the source
of opposition (3.22; 7.1), and is subject to Isaiah's condemnation
(7.6 f.). It is the city putting Jesus to death (10.32, 33; 11.1, 11, 15, 27;
15.41), whose temple awaits destruction (13.2) and desecration (13.14).³
The Marcan term for 'crowd' is a secular term (ὄχλος), while he
avoids the term λαός, which is rendered sacred in the LXX as the designation of the chosen people. The latter term is rare in Mark (con-

¹Mark makes no distinction between 'all' and 'the crowd'; in 2.4 the same
group is called 'the crowd' which in 2.12 is called 'all'; cf. 9.15: 'all the
crowd'. When there is no specific subject ('they'), the same vague chorus is
sometimes intended, apparently without further reflection: 7.37 refers to the
crowd of v. 33; similarly the parallel passage 5.42 may refer to the 'tumult'
(v. 39) of 'all' (v. 40), rather than to the intimate circle actually present.
²Lohmeyer, *Galiläa und Jerusalem*, 26–36, avoids this antithesis between the
twelve and what he assumes to be a definition of Galilee by saying that the
calling of the twelve 'strengthens' the Church Jesus has founded in Galilee.
Apart from the fact that this verse supports the small definition of Galilee
rather than Lohmeyer's large boundary, the whole section presents Jesus as
avoiding the crowd (3.7, 9, 13), not strengthening the Church. The way in
which Lohmeyer avoids the other negative attitudes toward Galilee in Mark
(6.1–6), and reads an emphasis upon Galilee into positive Marcan contexts
(mission of the twelve; Peter's confession; the transfiguration) is equally
artificial. Lohmeyer assumes *a priori* that Jesus' audiences are holy, but this
logic is refuted in 2.13–17. Cf. also John 1.5, 11. Lohmeyer's embarrassment
with the Marcan material is evident in his creation of a 'Galilean secret'
corresponding to the messianic secret.
³Cf. Lohmeyer, *Galiläa und Jerusalem*, 29, 33–34.

trast Matt. and Luke), occurring in the LXX usage only in a quotation *in malam partem* against the Pharisees and scribes as 'hypocrites' (7.5 f.), and in the secular sense in 14.2.[1] To this absence of positive designations for the chorus there corresponds a series of negative characterizations: 'the many who are coming and going' (6.31); 'those who are weeping and wailing' (5.38); 'this adulterous and sinful generation' (8.38);[2] 'unbelieving generation' (9.19).[3] The fascinated crowds who surround Jesus are clearly not looked upon with favour by Mark.

One must conclude that Mark's norm of piety is not to be found in the concept of the numinous, in either its awesome or its fascinating aspect. If the one attitude is insufficient because it tends to separate Jesus from history, the other tends to confuse him with history, so that Jesus himself withdraws from the mass scenes (1.35; 3.9, 13; 4.1, 35; 5.40; 6.31, 45; 7.33; 8.13; 9.2, 28, 30). Thus Mark's reservations with regard to the numinous correspond to the limits of his understanding of history: eschatology, Jesus and the Spirit are not aloof from history, but rather enter history and create history; but they are not immanent forces which develop out of the present evil aeon as its potentiality. Rather, they must 'come' from heaven at a certain time and place, not as the perfection of the present evil aeon, but as the beginning of its end.

B. FAITH AND UNDERSTANDING

If one is to take seriously Mark's specific exhortations 'not to fear' (5.36; 6.50; 16.6; cf. also 13.7), then one must look to his accompanying positive statements for his preference in religious attitudes. 'Cowardice' is contrasted with 'faith' during the storm (4.40). Jairus on hearing of his daughter's death is admonished; 'do not fear, just

[1] Cf. Strathmann, *TWNT*, IV, 49–52.

[2] Cf. Hauck, *TWNT*, IV, 742, and Büchsel, *TWNT*, I, 661. The odd introduction of the 'crowd' v. 34 may find in this allusion its explanation.

[3] This designation refers less to the disciples, whose faith is not in question, than to the father, 'one of the crowd' (v. 17) whose presence had been emphasized vv. 14 f. For it is the father's faith which is the subject of discussion (vv. 23 f.) For the eschatological significance of this term cf. Str-B I, 641; IV: 2, 976 ff. Volz, *Die Eschatologie der jüdischen Gemeinde im neutestamentlichen Zeitalter*, 1934, 148, shows how this eschatological designation can be used of a historical situation.

believe' (5.36; cf. also vv. 33 f.). The 'astonishment' of Jesus' home town (6.2) is identified as 'disbelief' (6.6), just as the 'amazed' crowd of 9.15 is an 'unbelieving' generation (v. 19). It is obvious that 'faith' is one term which Mark chooses to designate the religious attitude preferable to that of awe. Similarly the 'amazement' at Jesus' walking on the water (6.50 f.) is explained: 'for they did not understand', for 'their hearts were hardened' (6.52). At the transfiguration Peter's inappropriate suggestion is explained: 'for he did not know what to say, for they were terrified' (9.6). In 9.32 'they did not understand the saying, and were afraid to ask him'. It is the same situation as 10.24, 26, where the disciples are 'amazed', but are unclear as to Jesus' teaching and ignorant as to how to be 'saved', whereas the 'faith' of the sick woman and of Bartimaeus 'saved' them (5.34; 10.52). It is clear that 'understanding' is closely associated with 'faith' in defining the religious attitude Mark advocates. Therefore an analysis of these two interrelated terms should provide a clarification of Mark's ideal of piety.

The importance of the attitude of 'faith' for Mark is evident from the fact that it is the attitude which Jesus calls forth and praises. Jesus reproaches 'disbelief' (4.40; 6.6; 9.19), exhorts to 'faith' (5.36; 11.22), and goes out of his way to attribute praiseworthy action to 'faith' (2.5; 5.34; 10.52).

When one asks what meaning the term 'faith' bears for Mark, one is first struck by the intimate association between 'faith' and the eschatological action constituting the Marcan history. The woman's act of touching Jesus' garments is an act of faith, and is welcomed as such by Jesus (5.34); the attitude of awe accompanied her misgivings (v.33), and, if dominant, would have prevented the action altogether. Therefore as the interrupted story of Jairus is resumed, Jairus is exhorted to 'faith' rather than 'fear' (v. 36), so that the action of Jesus can continue in spite of the apparent death of the daughter. The association of 'faith' and Jesus' action is negatively accentuated in his home town, where he can hardly perform any 'mighty deeds' because of their 'unbelief' (6.5 f.). The importance of the attitude of 'faith' is such as to attribute to it, rather than to Jesus, the cure, 2.5; 5.34; 10.52. Similarly in 9.23, the issue is shifted from Jesus to the faith of the epileptic's father, so that the power is attached to the faith: 'Everything is possible to him who believes' (9.23). This power of faith to bring about the action of God is discussed thematically after the withering of the fig tree (11.22–24).[1]

Mark's interpretation of the attitude of 'faith' does not consist simply in its relation to action, but includes also a relation to knowing. The verb is transitive and the noun has a referential aspect: 'Faith' is 'in the gospel' (1.15) or 'in God' (11.22). One 'believes that what one says will happen', or 'that you received', and believing corresponds to praying (11.23 f.). 'Believing' also corresponds to saying that John the Baptist is 'from heaven' (11.31). It is an act of recognition, to be denied to false Messiahs (13.21), but which would be granted to Jesus as 'Christ King of Israel' if he would come down from the cross (15.32). Those who are 'Christ's' are called 'believers' (9.41 f.), so that 'believer' becomes a Christian self-designation presupposing some profession of Jesus as Christ. From this survey it is clear that Mark has no single person or act as the object of faith, and no specific credal statement as the content of faith.[2] Rather it is faith in the action recorded in the Marcan history, irrespective of whether the language refers to God causing the action, Jesus as able to perform it, the gospel proclaiming it, or prayer calling for it. Therefore while faith as action leads to the synonym, 'take courage' (6.50; 10.49), faith as knowing leads to the synonym 'follow'. This is such a typical description of the disciples' attitude (1.18; 2.14f.; 3.7; 5.24; 6.1; 10.52; 14.54; 15.41) that it becomes a technical designation of the disciples (10.32; cf. 9.38), and takes on symbolic theological significance (10.21, 28, 32, 52; 14.54; cf. also 8.34). It never loses its concrete relation to the history of Jesus, but is reserved by the early Church for those who 'followed' him during his earthly life.[3]

The aspect of 'knowing' which inheres in Mark's interpretation of

[1]This power of faith cannot, from Mark's point of view, be psychologized as the therapeutic value of confidence. Those whose faith is discussed are sometimes (2.5; 9.19, 23 f.) not the invalids themselves. The few miracles Jesus does in spite of unbelief are such as would, from the psychological viewpoint, require faith (6.5 f.), while the primary discussion of wonder-working faith (11.22–24) is treating not of healings open to psychological interpretation, but rather of miracles in the world of nature. In 2.5 faith effects the forgiveness of sins, not the cure.

[2]Cf. Martin Werner, *Der Einfluss paulinischer Theologie im Markusevangelium*, 106–18, where Mark's view of faith is distinguished from Paul's theologically fixed concept of 'faith in Christ'.

[3]Cf. Kittel in *TWNT*, I, 214.

'faith' recalls its close association to the term 'understanding'. When one investigates the Marcan usage of the latter term it becomes evident that it does not fall outside the scope of the term 'faith', nor does it even shift the Marcan ideal of piety away from the action aspect to the knowing aspect of 'faith'. Rather 'understanding' holds a centre of balance between the two aspects of 'faith'.

There are in Mark two things which are not 'understood': the feedings (6.52; 8.17, 21) and the parables (4.12; 7.14). In neither of these cases is it really a matter of comprehending intellectually a doctrine. The feedings are actions, not teachings (the incidental instructions *are* understood), and misunderstanding reveals itself in a kind of action; amazement at Jesus walking on the water (6.51), and concern about bread in the boat (8.14, 16). This action is a confused reaction to Jesus, failing to recognize in him—through the feedings—the action of God in history. In the parables too the problem of understanding is not intellectual, but existential: the 'parable' of what defiles (7.17) calls for 'understanding' (7.14, 18), but the interpretation consists less in adding any new insight to the discussion of vv. 1–14 than in pressing home a conclusion ('cleansing all foods' v. 19) which was difficult for some to accept. Similarly the 'parable' of the fig tree (13.28) is more an exhortation than an instruction, and the interpretation (v.29), in view of its vagueness, serves more as a concluding exhortation than as a clarification of details. Two parables are apparently understood intellectually (3.23; 12.1, 12) but repudiated existentially, so that the hearers are rejected (3.29; 12.12).

If Mark does not associate the problem of 'understanding' with that of intellectual clarification, he does associate it with the problem of 'hardness of heart' (6.52; 8.17).[1] This agrees with Mark's general view that the opponents of Jesus suffer from 'hardness of heart' (3.5; 10.5). Thus the problem of 'understanding' is removed from either an intellectual or a psychological context, and is endowed with the theological overtones which accompany the idea of 'hardness of heart' in the Old Testament history of God's people.[2]

---

[1] This term does not occur with regard to the parables, but its equivalent OT expression used in 8.18 of the feeding occurs in 4.12 of the parables: 'seeing they see and do not know, and hearing they hear and do not understand.' In the OT context (Isa. 6.9 f.), reference is made specifically to hardening (lit. 'fattening') of the heart (cf. Matt.).

[2] Cf. K. L. and M. A. Schmidt, *TWNT*, V, 1024–32.

The thematic discussion of the problem of 'understanding' takes place in terms of a discussion of understanding parables (ch. 4.) The first and longest parable is intended to explain the problem of understanding 'parables' as such (4.10–13): 'You do not know this parable, and how will you know all the parables?' The chapter as a whole is concerned with two levels of 'hearing': one is 'hearing but not understanding' (4.12); the other is the 'hearing' for which the chapter repeatedly calls (vv. 3, 9, 23, 24; cf. 7.14). This motif of two levels of understanding finds expression also in the repeated withdrawal from the 'outsiders' (4.11) to privacy for the interpretation (vv. 10, 33 f.; cf. 7.17). The interpretation of the first parable (vv. 14–20) is devoted to an explanation of these two levels: the superficial level, called 'seeing' and 'hearing' (v. 12), is exemplified by those who 'hear' the word but then fall away (vv. 15, 16, 18). The deeper level, called 'knowing' and 'understanding' (v. 12), is itself the objective of the interpretation (v. 13), and is exemplified by the fourth example: 'These hear the word and receive it and bear fruit thirtyfold and sixtyfold and a hundredfold' (v. 20). Most illuminating are Mark's explanations for the two levels: progress from the first to the second level is blocked by the cosmic enemy of Christ, Satan (v. 15). His action is explained as 'tribulation and persecution on account of the word' (v. 17), 'the cares of the age and the deceitfulness of riches and the desires for the rest' (v. 19). The deeper level is given by God (v. 11),[1] and corresponds to the 'repentance' and 'forgiveness' (v. 12) for which the gospel calls (repentance: 1.4, 15; 6.12; forgiveness: 1.4; 2.5, 7, 9, 10; 3.28 f.; 11.25). Thus the struggle for 'understanding' is the inner aspect of the eschatological struggle between Satan and God constituting the history of Jesus.

When Jesus gives understanding to those 'who have eyes but do not see and ears but do not hear' (8.18; cf. 4.9, 12, 23, f.), he is engaged in the same activity as when he gives sight to the blind (8.22–26; 10.46–52) and hearing to the deaf (7.32–37; 9.14–29): 'He has done all things well; he even makes the deaf hear and the dumb speak' (7.37). Herein is confirmed the unity between the whole Marcan presentation of Jesus' history on the one hand and his evaluation of the attitude of 'faith' and 'understanding' on the other. It is therefore evident that we have identified Mark's ideal of piety. This ideal is an attitude orientated

[1]The passive form implies God as the agent. Cf. Jeremias, *The Parables of Jesus,* 12, 15.

in terms of the eschatological struggle and committed to the historical action of Jesus and the Spirit. Mark does not advocate a non-historical, mystical religiosity, but rather gives expression to a religious attitude which recognizes the historicity of human existence.

C. THE SOCIETY CREATED BY JESUS' ACTION

Mark's understanding of history has been characterized as an awareness of two history-making forces in conflict with each other. Therefore the action of the Spirit in Jesus and the Church is an aspect of history moving toward its goal, just as the régime of the present evil aeon is an aspect of history moving towards its end. Correspondingly Mark's religious attitude is one of historical commitment. However, the sporadic vertical actions of the Spirit and the alertness of the believer to his historicity do not fully justify the assertion that one has to do in Mark with Jesus' and the Church's *history*. For the term 'history' normally contains a sociological factor; it is the movement of a society or people This brings with it traditions and custom, and in the long run a culture. If Mark conceived of Jesus immanently, as a continuation of the present evil aeon, the sociological impact of Jesus' history would be submerged within first-century Judaism. If Mark conceived of Jesus' action as purely transcendent, anti-historical, one would not expect a sociological factor, but at most a cluster of individual ascetics. If however Mark does look upon Jesus and the Church as both eschatological and historical, one would expect to find indications of a historical society, with its customs, ethos and tradition. However, such objectified manifestations of a history, such a movement toward the universal, toward status, toward empirical evidence, stand in a certain tension with the spirituality of the forces at work in history. They are in tension with the non-objectivity of Mark's presentation of Jesus' history, and to the risk and existential commitment involved in a religious attitude of historicity. If in spite of this tension Mark proceeds to include such a sociological dimension in his presentation, this must be evaluated as a confirmation of his intention to present a *history* of Jesus (and the Church), as well as a definition of piety.

The oral material about Jesus came to Mark bearing two traits of primary significance for the problem of Jesus and society: the material was in disconnected units, and it represented Jesus as leading an itinerant way of life. These motifs are used by Mark to present the origin of an eschatological society. Mark makes the first feeble beginnings toward temporal and geographic connexion of the stories.[1] But he also exploits the absence of a geographic connexion to accentuate that Jesus comes from God.[2] The 'comings' of Jesus in 1.24, 38; 2.17; 10.45 far surpass in significance the antecedent geographic 'comings' of 1.21; 35; 2.13; 10.1 and take on (esp. 11.11) the eschatological significance of 'coming' (8.38; 9.1, 11, 12, 13; 10.30; 11.9 f.; 13.6, 26, 35–6; 14.62; 15.36). Similarly in Jesus' itinerant way of life ('passing by': 1.16, 19; 2.14) he calls upon people to 'follow' him (1.17, 20; 2.14) in a two-fold sense (1.17b, 20; 2.17). Thus a recurrent motif of the historical narration is that he is 'followed': by many tax-gatherers and sinners (2.15); by a multitude (3.7); by a crowd (5.24); by disciples (6.1); by women (15.41). Mark makes it clear that this 'following' assures an eschatological restoration in this age and eternal life in the age to come (10.28–31; cf. vv. 17, 21), i.e., entrance into the kingdom of God (10.23). Thus Jesus separates persons from their natural and historical setting, and introduces them into an eschatological existence of communion with himself.

This eschatological existence is not, however, a private relationship to Christ, but is an existence shared with a group of disciples. The follower is separated from one society and placed in another. This society is on the one hand the inevitable travel companionship of the itinerant way of life, and on the other hand a theologically understood relationship. They are 'the twelve', suggestive of the twelve tribes of Israel,[3] a title to which Mark draws specific attention only in the listing of the names (3.16–19). They are 'apostles' (i.e., 'emissaries' 6.30), but only in connexion with their mission (3.14; 6.7). Their function is primarily for Mark 'so that they could be with him' (3.14). Jesus is 'with the twelve' (11.11; 14.17), or the inner group (9.8; 14.67; cf. also 1.29), or the unidentified disciples (2.19; 3.7; 4.36; 8.10). Thus a technical term for discipleship arises: 'those with him' (5.40; perhaps 1.36); 'those going up with him' (15.41); to 'be with him' (5.18). The theological significance of this term is also evident from its frequency

---

[1]Cf. K. L. Schmidt, *Der Rahmen der Geschichte Jesu.*

[2]Already Schweitzer, *The Quest of the Historical Jesus,* pointed to the 'positive non-connexion' of the narratives, which he correctly interpreted as suggesting some 'supernatural' or 'dogmatic' meaning (334 f. of the 1950 edition).

[3]Cf. Rengstorf, *TWNT,* II, 325 f.

in the communion of the last evening (14.14, 17, 18, 20, 33), which is shattered by Judas 'with a crowd' (v. 43) and Peter 'with the guards' (v. 54), denying that he had been 'with the Nazarene Jesus' (v. 67).

Although the number and designation of those 'with Jesus' varies, this group is clearly distinguished from the crowd by Mark. They are distinguished from the crowd terminologically (2.15; 3.9; 5.31; 6.45; 8.34; 9.14; 10.46), or by special functions (3.9; 6.35, 41; 8.1, 6; 11.1), authority (9.38; 10.13), power (3.15; 6, 7, 12 f.; cf. also 9.18), or customs (2.18; 7.2 f.). A recurring motif is that Jesus withdraws from the crowd to be with the disciples (3.7–19; 6.31 f.). Usually this withdrawal is for the sake of special instruction, whose significance is thus accentuated: 4.10, 34; 7.17; 9.28, 33–35; 10.10, 32; 13.3. Therefore this society is the bearer of certain esoteric teaching (cf. also 10.23; 11.14). What 'men' say of Jesus is distinguished from what 'you' the disciples say (8.27 ff.), for the disciples possess the messianic secret. They also witness certain important events (1.29; 5.37; 9.2), especially in passion week (11.11; 14.17, 33). They observe the scene (14.3–9) which is to be reported 'wherever the gospel is preached into all the world'. They are instructed as to Jesus' death (8.31; 9.31; 10.32) and resurrection (9.9; 10.33; 16.7). Thus the new society is identified as the bearer of the *kerygma*.[1]

It is clear that this society is understood theologically by Mark. Its members are those to whom the eschatological redeemer has come. He has removed them from a worldly society and incorporated them into an eschatological society. As witness to Jesus' eschatological history, this society is defined as 'Christ's' (9.41).

D. THE ESCHATOLOGICAL COMMUNITY

Two of the points at which Jesus' followers were most rudely snatched from their historical settings by their eschatological faith were their family relationships and their table fellowships. Here the early Christian could sense quite existentially the reality of being de-historicized. Yet it is precisely here that Mark makes it clear that the history which has been lost is replaced by a new history.

[1] The rôle of the twelve in Mark is not such as to prove the existence of a 'twelve-source', as has been maintained by Eduard Meyer, *Ursprung und Anfänge des Christentums,* I, 135, ff. Cf. the critique by C. H. Turner, 'Marcan Usage: Notes, Critical and Exegetical, on the Second Gospel. VIII. "The Disciples" and "the Twelve",' *JTS*, XXVIII (1926–7), 22–30.

Jesus had to break with his own family (3.19b–21, 31–35; 6.1–6). James and John forsook their father Zebedee (1.20), and the departure from Capernaum (1.36) took Peter and Andrew from their home (1.29–31). Such a disruption of family ties will characterize the end (13.12), when 'brother will betray brother to death and the father his son, and children will rise against their parents and have them put to death'. The new aeon will have no marriage (12.25). When the rich man is called upon to sell his property and follow Jesus in order to have 'eternal life' or the 'kingdom of God' (10.17, 21, 23–26), the latent theological significance of this sacrifice bursts into the open: Peter had 'left all' to 'follow' Jesus (10.28); it was for Jesus' sake and the gospel's (v. 29).

This leads to the thematic discussion of the eschatological replacement for the loss (10.30). The replacement is not simply the non-historical existence of the (still future) aeon to come, but first of all a new society: 'a hundredfold houses and brothers and sisters and mothers and children and fields'. The historicity of this society is accentuated by locating it 'now in this time' (i.e., within the present evil aeon). All that is listed as lost in one society (v. 29) is regained in the other a hundredfold.[1] Similarly the lists of Jesus' spiritual family (3.34 f.) are equally extensive with the lists of his natural family (3.31 f.); 'mother and brothers'; 'brother and sister and mother'. Therefore we do not have to do with an ultimate break with society, but only with the question (3.33) as to 'who is my mother and brothers'. This new society conforms to Mark's understanding of the history of the interim as a struggle: over against the blessings stands the promise of 'persecutions' (10.30)[2]

[1]The omission of the father is intentional in the same way as is that omission in the remarkably complete listing of Jesus' natural (3.31 f.; 6.3) and spiritual (3.33–35) family. God is the father of Jesus (8.38; 14.36) and Jesus is his son ([1.1]; 1.11; 3.11; 5.7; 9.7; 12.6; 14.61; 15.39), so that the two bear these titles absolutely (13.32). But Jesus speaks to the disciples of 'your father which is in heaven' (11.25), so that the gap in both Jesus' and the Christian's spiritual family is filled by God himself.

[2]If the general Jewish outlook was more historical than the Greek, by the fact that the Jew envisaged a goal of history, the Christian was even more historical, by the fact that his goal is itself historical during the interim. This verse avoids both the pessimism latent in the Greek view of history and the naive utopianism and self-glorification latent in the Jewish view. Cf. the criticisms of this verse (cited by Taylor, *Comm.*) by the Greek-thinking Clement of Alexandria and Julian the Apostate, and by the Jewish-thinking chiliasts.

The replacement of the natural family by the spiritual family is not in itself the non-historical existence 'like the angels', where 'they neither marry nor are given in marriage' (12.25). Rather Christian existence includes the monogamy of the garden of Eden (10.6). Jesus defends the integrity of the home (7.10–13; 10.2–12), yields to the requests of parents for their children (5.21 ff.; 7.24 ff.; 9.14 ff.), accepts the parents' faith for the cure of the children (5.36; 7.28; 9.24; cf. 1.31), grants to the parents the privileges of disciples (5.40), and sends cured persons home (2.11; 5.19; 8.26). Blood relationships among Christians are not ignored: 1.16, 19; 3.17; 5.37; 15.21, 40. However these relationships are relativized in terms of new Christian relationships; Peter has been separated from Andrew and associated with James and John (3.16–18; 5,37; 9.2; 13.3; 14.33);[1] James and John become 'sons of thunder' (3.17);[2] for the twelve apostles themselves replace the twelve patriarchs and make possible the interracial Marcan Church. The natural society is not an absolute, but must be reformed in terms of the spiritual society. In this sense the Christian family is for Mark a historical reality which has become eschatological. It can serve as a norm not for destroying other history, but for restoring it and directing it toward its goal.

Table fellowship is the other place where Mark shows a clear awareness of the separation from one history, society, custom and culture, and the entrance into another history, which also has its customs, society and ethical principles.

Mark's presentation of table fellowship is particularly useful in interpreting his understanding of his own history, since these passages reveal more clearly than most their *Sitz im Leben* in the early Church. The fact that table fellowship presented various problems for the early Church is evident from such passages as Gal. 2; I Cor. 8–11; Acts 6. The discussion of fasting (2.19 f.) refers specifically to the time of the Church. The debate concerning purification before meals (7.1 ff.) is clearly presented from the Christian, not from a Jewish context (v. 3). The last supper (14.22–25) is obviously the Church's eucharist (cf. I Cor. 11.23–26). The request of James and John (10.35–45), in view

[1]The order in 1.29 is an exception required by the narrative: 'into the house of Simon and Andrew with James and John.'
[2]Their blood relationship is emphasized precisely where it becomes a harmful factor (10.35).

of its eucharistic motifs (sitting beside Jesus; drinking his cup; serving; his life a ransom for many), may reflect eucharistic difficulties such as those of I Cor. 11.27–34. But also the two feedings of the multitude (6.34–44; 8.1–9, 14–21) are eucharistic.[1] Therefore it is evident that Mark's presentation of table fellowship reflects his understanding of his own situation.

Mark's table fellowship is for him a sacred, eschatological society. The eucharist is the fellowship of the interim, looking back upon Jesus' death (14.22–24; 10.38 f. 45), and forward to the *parousia* (14.25). It is the communion of the eschatological 'covenant' (14.24). Jesus feeds his Church miraculously and superabundantly (6.34 ff.; 8.1 ff.), and the 'Son of Man' feeds his disciples as the Lord of the eschatological Sabbath (2.23–28).[2] Just as feasting is in the presence of the eschatological bridegroom, fasting is in terms of his absence (2.19 f.). Therefore it is evident that this table fellowship is not a secular or peripheral part of Mark's experience, but rather a sphere where the eschatological reality is the formative factor.

Now it is this eschatological table fellowhip which displays most clearly the concomitant trappings of historical reality. It has its own customs: Its Sabbath practices are different from the Jewish tradition (2.23 ff.; 3.1 ff.), and in the first instance with regard to eating. It has its own fasting customs, outwardly parallel to Judaism, but understood in a new way (2.18–20; 14.25), and perhaps observed on a different day.[3]

---

[1]Pfleiderer, *Primitive Christianity*, II, 25 ff., points to the eucharistic feeding of the multitude in John 6.51–58; the five loaves and two fishes of early eucharistic paintings; the function of the deacons in the love-feast as described by Justin Martyr; the evening hour, at the close of the discourse, with the people reclining in orderly ranks and companies; and the eucharistic language in the blessing on the bread. Riesenfeld, *Jésus transfiguré*, 321, has shown that this last parallel is not coincidental, by illustrating how the similar wording of Mark 2.26 (and Luke 6.4) departs from that of I Kgdm., 21.6 (LXX) in the direction of the eucharistic phraseology. The absence of the cup does not argue against this interpretation, but rather recalls the 'breaking of bread' of Acts, 2.42, 46; 6.1–6 (cf. Lohmeyer, 'Das Abendmahl in der Urgemeinde', *JBL*, LVI [1937], 228 ff.). Compare also the meals of the Qumran sect, in the *Manual of Discipline*
[2]Cf. Lohmeyer, 'Vom urchristlichen Abendmahl', *TR*, n.F., IX (1937), 203.
[3]The phrase 'on that day' may allude to Friday as the day of Christ's death, in contrast to the Monday and Thursday fasts of the stricter Pharisees (cf. Luke 18.12; *Didache* 9.1). So Holtzmann, *Die Synoptiker*, 3. Aufl.; Gulin, *Die Freude im Neuen Testament*, 2, n. 1; Lohmeyer (*Comm.*); Klostermann (*Comm.*), with doubts. Lagrange (*Comm.*) holds that the allusion is too vague.

It has the custom of eating with unwashed hands, while the Jews observe the tradition of ceremonial cleansing before meals (7.2–5). This is cited as merely one point at which the Christian custom no longer follows the Jewish tradition (7.4).

Some of the instances where Christian custom varies from Jewish custom are of ethical significance; Jewish divorce regulations are rejected (10.2–12). The Corban subterfuge is rejected (7.9–13). The immoral scribal way of life, including its mealtime customs, is rejected (12.38–40). Similarly the gentile custom of 'lording it over' inferiors is rejected, and here too within the context of the Christian table communion, where 'service' is the ideal (10.42–45; cf. 9.35). The terms 'serve' and 'servant' retain their two-fold significance of waiting on tables (1.13, 31; 15.41) and of ethical service (10.45).[1] 'Compassion' predominates at the two miraculous feedings (6.34; 8.2; cf. 5.43; 9.41). Therefore the rejection of immoral custom leads to new ethical custom. For the Christian is not left to the *ad hoc* guidance of the Spirit for his ethical conduct, but is supplied with a warning *Lasterkatalog* such as was current in the Jewish and Hellenistic cultures of the day: 'evil thoughts, fornication, theft, murder, adultery, coveting, wickedness, deceit, licentiousness, an evil eye, slander, pride, foolishness' (7. 21f.)— as well as with the ten commandments (10.18 f.). These general ethical maxims are significant not only because their observance makes communal life possible, but also because the existence of generally valid ethical principles gives to the Marcan ethic a cultural in addition to its existential aspect.

The Marcan table fellowship is also involved in the correct definition of its constituency. Its policy of inclusiveness is attested on all sides: it admits 'tax-gatherers and sinners' (2.13 ff.); the eucharist is for the 'many' (14.24; 10.45);[2] the Syrophoenician woman is after all 'fed' (7.25–30).[3] The emphasis upon 'the children's crumbs' (7.28) has as its parallel the emphasis in both miraculous feedings on the quantity of

[1]Cf. Beyer, *TWNT*, II, 92.

[2]J. Jeremias, *The Eucharistic Words of Jesus,* 123–5, demonstrates that 'many' accentuates inclusiveness, not exclusiveness, and that this inclusiveness envisages specifically the gentiles (146–52). Cf. also Lohmeyer, 'Das Abendmahl in her Urgemeinde', *JBL*, LVI (1937), 227.

[3]The delay seems to reflect the pattern 'first the Jew and then the Greek', which is the flag under which the Pauline inclusiveness could be carried through (Rom. 1.16; 2.9 f.; Matt. 10.5 f.; 28.19; Acts 1.8).

broken pieces left over (6.43; 8.8). This aspect of the two feedings is brought forward as what is to be 'understood' (8.14–21).[1] The miracle of the multiplied food points to the miracle of the Church, that the eschatological reality is sufficiently inexhaustible to make possible a society open to all humanity.

It has become clear that Mark sees eschatological existence in terms of the life of a society which is sufficiently historical to have assumed already in Mark's time some of the cultural and traditional aspects of a historical organism. This society has its ethos, its *mores*, its constituency. Furthermore, each of these is for Mark rooted in the history of Jesus, and envisaged in eschatological perspective. This is not to say that these more mundane aspects of historical existence are central in Mark's understanding of history; but they do indicate that Mark's understanding of Christian existence consists in an understanding of history: the history of Jesus and the history of the Church.

[1]The association between the Syrophoenician's 'crumbs' and these 'broken pieces' is accentuated by the fact that these two passages correspond to each other in the doublet: 6.34–7. 23 and 8.1–26. Cf. the chart by Klostermann, *Comm.* Other associations between the feedings and the inclusion of gentiles have been observed; the twelve baskets for the twelve apostles, and seven for the hellenistic deacons (Acts 6.1–6; so Lohmeyer, 'Das Abendmahl in der Urgemeinde', *JBL*, LVI [1937], 235 ff.; cf. also Klostermann, *Comm.*); the inclusion of the doublet so as to represent the tradition of the two branches of the Church (so Sundwall, *Die Zusammensetzung des Markusevangeliums,* 50); the location in the Decapolis (cf. G. H. Boobyer, 'The Miracles of the Loaves and the Gentiles in St. Mark's Gospel', *SJT*, VI [1953], 78 ff.).

INDEX TO AUTHORS

Messel, N., 28 n., 46 n.
Meyer, E., 80 n.
Michaelis, W., 55 n.
Morgenthaler, R., 24 n.

Nestle, E., 22

Oepke, A., 11 n.
Oldshausen, H., 24 n.
Ott, H., 17 n.
Otto, R., 30 n., 68 n., 69 n., 71 n.
Overbeck, F., 18 f., n.

Pfliederer, O., 83 n.
Procksch, O., 36 n.

Raschke, H., 10
Rawlinson, A. E. J., 11 n.
Rengstorf, K. H., 79
Riesenfeld, H., 47 n., 83 n.
Ritschl, A., 8
Robinson, J. M., 32 n., 47

Schmidt, K. L., 12 f., 14 n., 16 n.,
    19 n., 25 n., 76 n., 79 n.
Schmidt, M. A., 76 n.
Schniewind, J., 13, 22 n.
Schweitzer, A., 8 n., 9, 79 n.

Schweizer, E., 29 n.
Sevenster, G., 50
Stauffer, E., 40 n., 48 n.
Strack-Billerbeck, 25 n., 48 n., 40 n.,
    73 n.
Strathmann, H., 73 n.
Strauss, D. F., 7
Sundwall, J., 85 n.

Taylor, V., 22 n., 81 n.
Troeltsch, E., 16 n.
Turner, C. H., 80 n.

Volkmar, G., 11
Volz, P., 73 n.

Weber, F., 46 n.
Weiss, B., 57 n.
Weiss, J., 57 n.
Weisse, C. H., 8 n.
Wellhausen, J., 9, 10 n., 23 n.
Wendland, H. D., 31
Werner, M., 11, 75 n.
Westcott-Hort, 22
Wilke, C. G., 7 n.
Windisch, H., 25 n.
Wrede, W., 9, 11 f., 14, 35 n., 38 n.,
    69 n.

88

INDEX OF BIBLICAL REFERENCES